Long Trot

JOHN O' GROATS TO LAND'S END
2007
GRANT NICOLLE

First published by Amazon - June 2015
002

Copyright © Grant Nicolle, 2015

Printed on demand by Amazon

ISBN: 978-1503338692

Foreword by Amy Williams MBE

"I was privileged to have met Grant in 2010, after competing in the Vancouver Olympics. He had heard about my love of horses, and had invited me to visit and ride some of the wonderful horses of The King's Troop in Woolwich, London. Whilst out riding 'William' the huge black horse I'd been given for the day, Grant had told me about his long ride across Britain.

It's been wonderful now to read "Long Trot 2007" about his adventurous ride on Marv, his horse, and how together they completed the huge task of riding through our country. Listening to the challenges and tasks thrown at them was inspiring and refreshing. Next time I think I need to get an invite to join in!"

With Amy at The King's Troop's new barracks in Woolwich

Amy Williams is no stranger to challenges. After winning Great Britain's only gold medal at the 2010 Vancouver Winter Olympics, she has been busy as a rally GB co-driver, excelled in the Arctic survival show '71 Degrees North', survived Discovery Channel's 'Alone in the Wild', featured as a co-presenter on Ski Sunday and is soon to be part of Channel 5's 'The Gadget Show'. Amy has had a passion for horses all her life and is a very gifted and natural rider.

Notes on Long Trot 2007

Contents

Background

Preparing for the trip

Week 1

Week 2

Week 3

Week 4

Week 5

Week 6

Week 7

Week 8

Week 9

Week 10

Week 11

Week 12

Summary of route / miles

Glossary

Acknowledgements

Background

In my last year in the Army, serving as a Captain in the King's Troop Royal Horse Artillery (RHA), I had the privilege of being part of the 2003 Edinburgh Military Tattoo. This enabled me to ride at the front of a procession of Army horses towing World War One field guns up the historic Royal Mile (to the delight of the many tourists). On each performance night, our military cavalcade was held just outside the Castle esplanade to wait for our turn to make an entrance into the Tattoo arena. One night, whilst waiting to go in, as I was sitting high on my 18 hand charger in the half darkness, on the ancient cobbles surrounded by period buildings, wearing traditional RHA uniform with sword in hand, I felt like I had been sent back in time to many centuries earlier. To be in uniform and mounted just outside Edinburgh Castle set off my imagination of what it must have been like to travel on horses in centuries past. This was the occasion where the seed of the idea of the ride started.

Taking the salute at the Tattoo on 18hh Able

Three years later, in the autumn of 2006, I decided that I would commit to travel from John o' Groats to Land's End with a horse. This expedition would put into practice elements of my previous military training and combine it with my passion for travel and exploring new places. The concept of the challenge was to travel solo with a horse and without the need of a following support vehicle or replacement horse. A hundred years ago this would not have been unusual, when horses were the main form of transport. Now that horses are being kept mostly for sport or recreational purposes, the myriad of bridleways that were once so well used now rarely see the quantity of hoof prints of yesteryear. Before I go into the details of the trip itself, and to help provide some context as to what contributed to my decision to undertake it, I will provide a summary on how I became interested in horses, and my relatively short history of riding both before and during my time in the Army.

My passion for horses started in Shropshire in the '90s, when Rob, a school friend, ran a livery yard near Bridgnorth. After telling him I was keen to learn to ride, he obligingly took me out for a few hacks. During the hacks he gave me tips on how to improve my riding as he was a qualified Assistant Instructor. I loved to ride fast, but realistically I had no real control. The equine theme continued soon after at Oxford Brookes University when I became quite keen on Caroline, a girl on my course, who owned and competed event horses. I was lucky enough to be invited down to stay at her family's estate in Hampshire. After some persuasion, Caroline agreed to take me out for a hack. During the ride I optimistically suggested we might canter around a stubble field. Very shortly after we started to canter Caroline rode over and grabbed my horse's reins, and I was unceremoniously brought back to a halt. She announced that I was too unskilled to be cantering on her horse, therefore the hack was effectively over and we returned "in walk" back to the yard. I was inwardly very disgruntled after been told that I was not proficient. This to me amounted to a personal challenge which would later help influence the direction of my career path.

After university, I joined the Army in 1997 and completed the Officers Commissioning Course at the Royal Military Academy at Sandhurst. From completing Sandhurst in spring 1998, I joined the Regiment of the Royal Artillery (RA). Now a Second Lieutenant, I attended the six month Young Officer's course at the Royal School of Artillery at Larkhill in Wiltshire. This was a great course (especially the social life) where around 20 of us were taught the specialist skills required to be an Artillery Officer.

As part of this military course we were expected to attend at least one traditional early morning riding lesson before breakfast each week. Most of the Young Officers (YOs) did not find this activity much fun, but Dave, Wardy and I absolutely loved the experience, often going twice a week by taking the places of other more reluctant YOs. On many occasions we would ride even when we had not been to bed, having been up socialising at the YO's bar until dawn. My riding came on a little, but I knew I still had a long way to go to be considered competent as demonstrated by another event.

One weekend I suggested to the Sergeant in charge of the RA stables that Dave and I were perhaps good enough to take two Army horses out for a hack onto the adjacent Salisbury Plain. The stables were only a few hundred metres from the perimeter fence, and from there it was open countryside, with no fences for miles. On the Plain there was also the RA racecourse, around which I was keen to gallop. Dave was not so confident and gave caution to the idea. However, I managed to persuade the Sergeant to lend us the horses. After receiving permission, we nervously tacked the horses up ourselves (having only just learnt how to do so) and were told the code for the lock on the gate to the Plain. Off we rode round

Larkhill camp looking for the said gate. We had forgotten to ask directions as to where the gate was.

My horse immediately got very excited about going on the hack and started jogging on the spot and frothing at the mouth. This worried me, as I had never experienced this sort of equine behaviour, and so when we came across a rugby field I naively thought that if I gave my horse a good canter round the pitch it might calm down a little. Little did I know! Off we went, galloping round and round the pitch with no brakes and little steering. Dave sat calmly in the middle of the pitch on his mellow horse watching me and suggesting that the hack might not have been such a good idea. He was right. I could not stop the speeding horse, and the situation felt dangerous. I ended up having to steer it at a very steep bank in the hope that it would just stop and not try and climb up it. Fortunately the horse did stop just long enough for me to jump off, and we began the walk of shame back to the stables. We were embarrassed even further as, just as we came to the yard, two young teenage girls were hacking out on similar horses and enquired if we were ok. I really needed to learn how to ride properly!

After the YO's course at Larkhill I was posted to my first regiment which was 7th Parachute Regiment Royal Horse Artillery (7 Para RHA), based in Aldershot. As an officer in 7 Para RHA you were required to pass P Company, which is an arduous 4 weeks physical selection process, then held in Catterick, Yorkshire. The main emphasis of this course is to test the robustness of one's physical stamina, courage and commitment. This is achieved by undergoing numerous long speed marches with 35lb bergens (military rucksacks) and weapon together with other physically demanding activities. It is designed to ensure that individuals have the self-motivation to endure physical hardship and also complete potentially unsavoury tasks such as jumping out of an aeroplane when required to do so. At the end of the course those that pass are awarded their maroon beret. I wore mine with pride upon my return to 7 Para RHA's Officers' Mess. Completing P Company and undertaking other similar arduous physical training exercises in my time in the Army certainly helped give me the confidence that I could complete the trip.

The last course I had to complete at 7 Para RHA was my jumps course. This was a 4 week parachute training course held at Royal Air Force (RAF) Brize Norton in Oxfordshire. My late father (then a Squadron Leader in the RAF) had just left Brize Norton as the Officer Commanding Military Training Flight (OCMTF) and he had, in his last month as OCMTF, given out parachute wings to the previous course (which included my Sandhurst platoon colleague Colin from 1 Para) just before my arrival. So I missed getting my wings from him by one course. My father (and our family) had been posted to RAF Brize Norton three times in total, and so I was very familiar with the air base and the surrounding area. It transpired that I would be returning there years later with a horse.

Having now earned my maroon beret and parachute wings, I was a fully-fledged officer in 7 Para RHA. Once established there, I soon found the local military stables in Aldershot town and started having lessons there. This was certainly an attempt to continue to improve my riding, and nothing to do with the appeal of the pretty female civilian riding instructor. However, the Ministry of Defence (MOD) were in the process of selling off the stables, so my time there was cut short.

During my time in Aldershot I was asked at short notice to be part of the Regiment's Modern Pentathlon team for the Army Championships, to be held at Sandhurst. 7 Para RHA ensured everyone's fitness levels were permanently kept high and I could just about sit on a horse, but had probably only show jumped once before, and I certainly had never fenced. Day one of the competition saw us complete the air pistol shooting which was being held in the squash court. I did not manage a good score as I had gone night clubbing to Guildford the night before, and my hand was still shaking. Then came the swim which we did ok at as a team of 3. Straight after lunch, we went to the gym where Craig (who had competed for Great Britain as a junior at Modern Pentathlon) showed me some basic fencing moves. I then managed to surprise some of the competitors with my unorthodox and unskilled fencing style, winning half my bouts. On Saturday night it was the Regiment's Summer Ball, and for once I laid off the booze as we were in a good position in the competition. On Sunday it was up early and into No.2 Dress jacket and breeches for the show jumping. I can remember being quietly confident about my chances, but having no clue really as to how to complete a round of show jumps properly. During the warm up I discovered that the horse I was allocated was massive and could clearly jump. When it was my time in the arena I somehow made it round the course with a few minor faults and actually crossed the finish, before my horse turned sharply and tried to jump another fence. The horse and I parted company. I took a bow, dusted my uniform down and walked out of the arena with the horse in hand. Fortunately my time still counted and I managed to gain a good amount of points for the team. After the run, 7 Para RHA went on to win the team event and I came 5th overall somehow, not bad for never having fenced or really show jumped. Despite this relative success it would have been a better result had I not fallen off.

Midway through my tour (of 3 years) at 7 Para RHA, I was asked to choose which regiment I wanted next as a posting. I had heard good things about The King's Troop RHA, which was a mounted ceremonial unit, based in St John's Wood, London. I had met some of their officers when I was recruiting officer for 7 Para RHA and they seemed a good sort. In 2000 I stayed at The King's Troop for 2 weeks in the summer on a short riding course. This course is held annually to promote riding in the military and also provides extra manpower for The King's Troop and some respite for Troop soldiers. The hours were long, the mucking out and stable management hard work, but for this effort we were rewarded by riding twice a day. It was this unique experience that helped me to decide that this was the posting I should apply for. When I told the Commanding Officer of my choice, I was warned that at my (relatively late) age in the Army, getting posted to The King's Troop was tantamount to career suicide, as it was outside mainstream gunnery. Despite his advice, I had made my mind up, and was fortunate to be accepted. I was duly posted there when my tour at 7 Para RHA ended. At least I should now be taught how to ride properly. Thanks Caroline.

After my posting to The King's Troop was confirmed, it was suggested that I go to Sandhurst and hack out with a King's Troop Bombardier (Artillery rank of Corporal) who worked at the stables there. He would also be able to help assess my riding ability and report back to the Troop. The Bombardier will remain nameless, but he very likely purposely mounted me on a horse which had just had a recent scare and was prone to bolting. As soon as we had walked into the Barossa training area at the Royal Military Academy Sandhurst (RMAS) and broke into a trot, my horse accelerated quickly and began galloping away with me. It was all I could do just to stay on. The Bombardier chased after me on his horse calling for me to "hang on in there". We galloped madly through the trees, where only a few years earlier I had been on exercise myself as an Officer Cadet. As we rounded a bend I saw a rapidly approaching platoon of Officer Cadets marching in formation. With no control, it was all I could do to shout "get out of the way!" whereby the Cadets unceremoniously and rapidly scattered off the forest track. I apologised to the directing staff as I sped through the swiftly emptied track. The horse finally became tired after about a mile and came back to a walk. The Bombardier caught up with me and told me he thought I did ok as I was still in the saddle. I am not sure that saddling me with that particular horse was a wise choice. Some test that was! On the plus side, I learnt that even on a runaway horse all is not lost.

In September 2001, I left 7 Para RHA to start my 6 month military riding instructor's course at Melton Mowbray in Leicestershire. The King's Troop send all their new officers on this course. The course is held at the Defence Animal Centre (DAC), which is the home of the Royal Army Veterinary Corps (RAVC). The DAC also has a vet hospital, the Army School of Farriery, the Military Dog Training School as well as the Army School of Equitation. The AMEC (Advanced Military Equitation Course) is an incredible course and it is a privilege to have completed it. The course runs once a year and has only twelve riders on it. The riders come from the Household Cavalry Mounted Regiment (HCMR), which is based in Knightsbridge Barracks (London), The King's Troop, RAVC and the Royal Mews. We had three from the Troop on the course and I was the only officer. The course was primarily for experienced riders who were sent there to be trained to be military riding instructors. The others on the course had all completed many years in the Army and could all ride to quite a good standard. I started the course as the least experienced by far.

The first day of the AMEC saw us all getting checked for our riding ability. We were taken by the instructors around the DAC's own cross country course. I was petrified, as I had only show jumped maybe three times before. Most of the young guys loved it, and somehow I managed to stay on and survive the first of many frightening experiences. There was a huge amount to learn just to close the gap with my peers on the course, but this was the right place to be taught.

A typical day's routine started early with mucking out, and then yard had to be swept spotless before heading back to the Mess for a shower and breakfast. Lessons started at 0900. We had three rides a day as well as lessons in the classroom and stable management in the yard. There was a large military forge co-located on the yard and they were always busy keeping the horses well shod. The equine section had a large number of resident fully trained Army horses which were looked after by a group of civilian female grooms. All these particular horses were capable of show jumping and cross country, but many also had some nasty equine habits - which would help teach us how to handle difficult horses. Some were prone to rearing or bucking (or both) and we soon learned each particular horse's bad traits. We were allocated two of these horses to ride every day for one week, and so when the list was read out naming our next two horses we would all hope not to have the really troublesome ones. As the course went on we discovered that some horses were great at cross country but would rear during flat work and military rides. Others were fine for everything except when in the show jumping arena, where some specialised in binning unsuspecting riders. I had my fair share of falls, but one unlucky chap broke his leg after landing badly from a fall whilst show jumping. We were then down to eleven.

As well as the two full trained horses we rode daily, in the first half of the course our 3rd ride was to be a half trained horse, which we were allocated and introduced to in the second week. Half trained horses are ones which have either only been backed and barely ridden, or have been sent to the DAC for re-schooling. I was given a horse called Beatrix, an older mare (twelve year old), who was safe but quite thick skinned and needing retraining (a fair description of me too). Our job with the half trained horses was to take these on and complete their training to enable them to be a fully trained horse. Thereafter they would be capable of going off to work in one of the many Army riding clubs in the UK and Germany.

At the half way point in the course there was a change; we rode one fully trained horse, one half trained horse and were given our remount horses. Remounts are the name for unbroken Army horses. Ours had been bought up to a year previously and had been living wild as a herd in the local fields up until this point. All had shaggy coats and two foot long manes. I was lucky again as my designated horse was a laid back gelding (who ended up in my Section at the Troop two years later). Our job with the remounts was to back them and teach them to walk, trot and canter and be able to jump a small number of show jumps. We had three months to complete this training. I thought this was a particularly interesting part of the course but some of the HCMR riders were given very wild horses in comparison to mine, and consequently there was some spectacular falls in the indoor school.

At the end of the course we each had to complete our military riding instructor assessment and also our British Horse Society (BHS) Assistant Instructor assessment. I was fortunate to pass both courses. The AMEC culminated in a one day event on our half trained horses. Beatrix and I never really clicked in the dressage and we got the lowest score. This was mostly down to me still not being able to work a horse softly into an outline. Beatrix then embarrassed me by resolutely refusing the first cross country jump in front of the whole course (as well as Mother and her partner Ken, who had come to see me pass out from the course). I managed to get her over eventually, completed the course and got round the show jumping to finish last in the one day event. Even though I had spent six months full time on an intensive riding course, I still had a lot to learn.

After completing my AMEC course, it was time to actually join the Troop in St John's Wood (or 'the Wood'). Once there, one of the first jobs I was asked to do during my handover period was to organise a national two week recruiting tour. I was given six horses, one field gun, ten soldiers, one horse box, one lorry and one Landrover to utilise. I had a month in which to plan the tour, using only a guide book listing all the UK's rural county shows. I called Show secretaries offering our services as a main ring attraction, and secured enough bookings to make up a tour. The itinerary took us from Cumbria to Devon via North Wales, Staffordshire and Shropshire. The recruiting tour was a great success in that we had no mishaps and we managed to display our one gun team in a thirty minute show to crowds of varying sizes. Our display commenced with a short demonstration of how the Troop trains a horse to work with the traces on. The single horse was then put back into team and the gun team walked, trotted and cantered round the ring. The gun was unhitched from the horses, a few blank rounds were fired before being re-hitched and them galloping out of the arena. I was on the microphone giving a running commentary for the team. As we were on a tight budget, we stayed in a variety of free accommodation provided by the shows which included tents, barns and barracks, with the horses often being stabled nearby at a local farm.

At two of the shows we were challenged to compete against the local riders in a hunt race which would take place in the main arena at the end of the show. This would be a great additional opportunity to highlight the equine skills of the Troop. Having no spare horses available for our displays, I accepted the challenge on the proviso that horses were provided by the show for our soldiers to compete on. This made the spectacle even more challenging as our soldiers would not have ridden the horses prior to the race and this made for a disadvantage. The hunt races included numerous jumps but key to our success was a requirement to dismount for a gate opening and then remount. All Troop soldiers can speedily mount from the ground with ease (by vaulting on) and it was with this advantage we managed to beat the locals using borrowed horses. The tour was interesting to organise and great fun to lead and be part of. I had been given an especially talented group of riders for the tour, which hopefully impressed people watching and made people consider joining up.

Once you were inside the gates at The Troop, time seemed to have stood still from early in the last century. The uniforms, saddles and bridles have hardly changed for almost a hundred years. The guns, limbers and traces still are exactly as they originally were when they were used in the First World War. It felt at times like one was working in a live military museum. The Troop is quintessentially about maintaining tradition and keeping exceedingly high standards (especially when it comes to polishing leather and shiny metal), and this can be a little strange when you are living in the 21st century. Reveille was sounded by trumpet at 0530 each day to initiate mucking out. The junior soldiers were sent out on morning exercise whilst the remainder stayed to conclude tidying the lines.

As Orderly Officer you were required to lead the morning exercise for 90 minutes round London. I liked to plan my routes well and try and take a different route each time. Favourites included going round Hyde Park, or a long trot up the hill to Hampstead. One Sunday morning I attempted and succeeded in taking a reduced exercise from the Wood over Westminster Bridge (which was very rarely achieved) and back in the allocated time. This required a large amount of trotting and the soldiers involved supporting the challenge. When morning exercise returned at 0800 the lines were immaculate and the trumpeter sounded the call for morning feed. Once the horses were fed the soldiers and officers then went for their breakfast. After breakfast soldiers returned to the lines to commence grooming, and the endless polishing of leather and metal for the next parade. The day sometimes involved further riding in the form of some show jumping or a military riding lesson. On other days the whole Troop would ride to Wormwood Scrubs to practice our formal display, both on the grass and on the all-weather surface there.

Officers, who were not on Orderly Officer duty, would be on their first charger by 0600, after walking through the lines at 0545 to ensure mucking out was progressing. As a Section Commander I was responsible for exercising two chargers daily. Officers could choose whether it was two flatwork sessions in the indoor or outdoor school, or a hack out into London. At the weekends we were lucky enough to be able to invite friends (who could ride) to join us for a hack out. It was a rare privilege to ride over Hampstead Heath, Primrose Hill or to go galloping down Rotten Row in Hyde Park. Now that the Troop has moved to Woolwich, I understand that the morning routine has changed so that morning exercise goes out after breakfast.

During my time at the Troop I was fortunate to ride on parade for: firing royal gun salutes in Hyde and Green Park; the Queen's birthday parade (Trooping of the Colour); Royal Windsor Horse show and other regional shows (including Sandringham and the Royal Welsh) and undertake the 4 o'clock Officer inspection at Horse Guards. To undertake the inspection, I rode in No.1 dress uniform from St John's Wood, through Oxford Circus onto the Mall and through to the small barracks on Whitehall. The inspection of the guard there was completed on foot, before remounting and riding back to the Wood generally though Regent's Park. On one particular return from the inspection I surprised a few sunbathers in the park who did not hear me cantering on the grass.

When not on military ceremonial duties, I was fortunate to be able to participate in many equine competitions including show jumping, cross country, hunter chasing, one day eventing and team chasing events. These activities were promoted to all at the Troop as they helped both horses and riders improve their skills. Officers were tasked with the organisation of the entries and logistics for the competitions. Over the winter months there was the added bonus of many days hunting to be had in Leicestershire, with some of Britain's well known hunts including the Belvoir, Cottesmore and Quorn. The Troop keeps a number of horses at Melton Mowbray over the winter specifically for hunting. This gives the horses a welcome break from the London routine and affords all ranks the chance to tackle big hedges.

For two weeks every year each Section would independently travel to seaside locations around Britain to allow the horses and soldiers to unwind. I chose to take Centre Section to Blackpool as there was an International League for the Protection of Horses (ILPH) centre at Penny Farm run by an ex-Sergeant from Centre Section, Tony Fleming. The horses thoroughly loved the camp, as they were turned out into the fields for some serious relaxing and equine socialising. As part of the camp we organised some cross country training round Penny Farm's own course. We also made the essential trip to the beach at nearby Lytham St Annes. After loading up 20 horses into one of the big horse artic lorries, we took them down to the wide open sands. Traditionally, saddles are not used on a beach ride and the horses knew what to expect. They were ridden 'in walk' down to one end of the beach and then we turned and raced them down the whole length of the beach bareback. We expected fun-filled carnage and we weren't disappointed. As we took off in gallop there were some immediate fallers, resulting in horses going off in all directions. The race was incredible fun, and as the few of us who actually made it to the end of the beach still mounted turned to witness the results, there were loose horses being rounded up everywhere and soldiers attempting to remount. Once back in a group we headed into the sea for the second part of the beach party, the swim. The horses loved the water and we managed to swim them as a group a short distance before riders began floating away from their mounts.

Near the end of my time at the Troop I was lucky enough to be chosen to be in charge of an amalgamated Section sent to be part of the Edinburgh Tattoo. Whilst in Edinburgh for the Tattoo, the horses were stabled in Holyrood Palace mews and the two field guns housed in what is now the Holyrood coffee shop. Our short part in the Tattoo each evening was insufficient daily exercise for the horses. So, as the Officer responsible, it was my job to lead out the daily morning exercise of horses. I chose the routes, so on different days I took the horses all over the city. The rides included Portobello beach, where we had the horses walking in the sea, and over the pass between Arthur's Seat and the crags. The Arthur's seat route in retrospect, was not the most sensible idea, as the soldiers each ride one horse and lead another. The footpath was quite narrow and the horses (which are mainly used to road exercise) suddenly needed to be as nimble as a fell pony, which they weren't. We had a great time in the City and it appeared that the general public and tourists in Edinburgh loved the horses. Edinburgh doesn't generally see horses in the city centre apart from the mounted police branch on patrol from their then base in Fettes, Stockbridge.

When I left the Army in 2003, I continued to ride where I could, managing to ride out on some point to point horses near Ludlow and at a race yard near Bridgnorth. I also managed to do some jousting at the weekends with a Shropshire based team who toured the country performing at small shows. During the jousting, for safety reasons, we weren't permitted to intentionally knock the opposing knight off his horse. It was secretly predetermined who would win each bout. The winner used a lance with a discreetly weakened end which would break in a safe manner after contact with the losing knight's shield. As I was the team's spare knight, I had the dubious privilege of riding the least trained horse. My first show didn't start well, we rode into the arena four abreast with our helmets on and carrying our colours on long standards. My horse then shied at the central rail, lurched sideways and I ended up on the deck with the horse cantering round on its own. This gave the crowd great amusement, to which I had no option but to smile, wave and walk off to get remounted for the jousts.

Finally, I headed back to Scotland where I was to make my home in Edinburgh.

In 2012 the King's Troop moved out of their home of St John's Wood (as their lease ran out) and were relocated in a new purpose built facility at George VI lines in Woolwich Garrison. Woolwich is the traditional home of the Royal Artillery, and I was fortunate enough to visit the Troop in October 2012 as part of a former Officer's lunch and tour. The visit evoked many emotions for me, as this is where I was dined in to the Royal Regiment of Artillery back in 1997. The starting place of my short Army career is now where the future of the King's Troop is. Although the facilities are better than the old barracks it does not replace the incredible sense of tradition and history that you felt when you entered the old gates on Ordnance Hill. I am glad I have seen where the horses and soldiers are now based, and am pleased that the new facilities are so good. I hope that the unit can survive the constant scaling back the MOD is undergoing. The fact that the horses will never be stabled in St John's Wood again makes my memories of the time I spent there even more special and unique.

That is the background of my link to and involvement with horses both in and out of the Army. I hope it maybe gives a flavour of the some of the experiences I have enjoyed and it may help explain a little why I decided to embark on this trip. The total amount of riding I have done is perhaps relatively little compared to many people who grow up riding, but I believe that I have managed to experience a wide variety of types of equestrian activities, and have had the good fortune to ride a large number of various types of horses.

Preparing for the trip

It was 2006, and my job as a project manager with the construction company Mace was becoming a tad frustrating. Mace had won the contract to build new Aldi stores all over Scotland and I had already been involved in managing the construction of three of them. The downside of this contract was the necessity of being relocated in distant parts of the country during each build. I was keen on actually spending some time in Edinburgh (where I lived) and so managed to convince Mace to relocate me to work on an RBS refurbishment project in central Edinburgh. This move gave me the time I needed to make plans. In the autumn I made up my mind to undertake the trip which would begin the following spring. To ensure that I didn't back out of the plan I started telling a few people of my idea. Most thought I was crazy and that it would never happen, which was not a very reassuring reaction, except one key person. I had met Fiona through Matt, a good friend of mine who was a Captain in the locally based Royal Scots Regiment. Matt and I had become friends during our time working in the 2003 Edinburgh Tattoo. During the Tattoo period, Matt had ridden out with us on one of our morning exercises round Arthur's Seat, the day the BBC team took footage of us for the Tattoo.

Fiona had grown up with horses and has an amazingly driven personality. She thrives on challenges and once I had shared my idea with her she was fully in support of the plan. It was with this crucial support that I then started my research into the feasibility of the scheme. I bought all the books on travelling by horse I could find, and then read them carefully, making notes on the issues faced by equine adventurers. I used Google to investigate who else may have done anything similar. I discovered that a certain Vivian Wood-Gee had completed the trip with her daughter a few years previously. Managing to track her down, I called her up to seek some advice. She kindly invited me down for supper at her farmstead in the Borders, where I asked hours of questions about her trip and the issues that arose. It was great to meet Viv and meeting her in person was very useful as it gave me the renewed confidence that the trip was achievable and that I certainly should carry on with the planning and logistics.

The trip as I saw it would be just me and one horse. No horsebox or support vehicle and no spare horse. I weighed up other options, but I still came back to the same plan. One sensible older horse, with strong legs and good weight carrying ability should do the trick. I would need saddle bags for my gear and equipment to look after the horse. Maps were needed, lots of them. I bulk bought all the necessary 1:50,000 Ordnance Survey (OS) maps on line and also some excellent OS 1:250,000 planning maps of the UK. From the planning maps (I needed 6 to cover the route) I first planned the outline of the route, before going into the detailed planning stage. My start point was to be John o' Groats. Vivien had suggested that I go from north to south because this meant I would miss the Highland's notorious midge season, a logic which I wholly concurred with. Thus I set the target start date as the 1st of May 2007 and the completion date to be approximately 12 weeks later (around 80 days). What was upmost in my mind during the planning was that if the horse became ill or injured at all (or for more than a couple of days at most), the trip was essentially over. I therefore kept the daily mileage to a sensible level. I reasoned upon averaging 20 miles a day for 6 days a week. This was to allow for a compulsory rest day for both the horse and me on a Sunday. I then poured over the planning maps and pencilled out a route of a series of 20 mile days (staying off the main roads) ensuring that I ended each day in a village which had at least a pub in it. My theory was that I would most likely be able to find a field for the horse, and I could then be sure to get food in the pub if required. This theory was to be well tested in the south west of England. So it was with this system of route planning I sketched out my rough route for the trip.

The overall mileage was working out at approximately 1100 miles and the route managed to incorporate seeing and staying with a large number of family and friends along the way. I had purposely designed the route to take in anyone I knew so that I could share the trip with them. This meant the route did take a slightly longer distance than if I was just heading straight to Land's End.

To do this trip I would need to get agreement from my employers Mace. My leave allowance would not stretch to this amount of time off. I had convinced myself that if they would not let me go I would hand in my notice to do the trip. Potentially quite a career risk, but one worth taking. Thus resolved, I duly outlined my plan to my boss and to my surprise they fully supported me. I was allowed to use all my annual leave for part of the trip and take an unpaid leave of absence for the remainder time. Superb, now we were on.

All the planning in the world would mean nothing without a good horse, so it was crunch time. I needed to buy a horse fast, and then get it fit for the trip. It was now November/December 2006, and I had only 4 or 5 months before the start. Fiona and I were looking through the local Scottish & Northern Equestrian classifieds to see if we could spot a potential candidate. There were so few horses advertised for sale that I began to get worried that I would need to go across the border to source a capable mount. In the ads there was only one potential horse worth a look, a 16hh 12 year old Clydesdale cross. He certainly looked strong, so I headed out to East Linton to have a look. I met Marvellous (or Marv) for the first time and my initial thoughts were; he's not a looker but he clearly had a strong personality (possibly a fair description of me too...). I took him out for a test ride, firstly in the outdoor school where he was as smooth as can be in walk, trot and canter and overall very relaxed. I then asked if I could take him round the stubble fields to see his speed work. I was told that he can be a bit fresh out in the fields, and so it turned out. Marv changed from being a soft school horse into a feisty bucking bronco as he sped round the field doing his best to unseat me. I loved the energy and spirit he showed and decided that he was the horse I was looking for.

I was told by the seller that he had a noticeable lump on his girth, and so I booked a 5 star vet check before I would conclude a purchase. A few days later, I attended the vetting, ending with the vet and I discussing Marv and the intended trip. Marv was fully sound but the girth lump was a real concern for the length of trip planned. We agreed that if I bought Marv then the lump would need to be removed. This was a real risk as we didn't know if the lump (or potential sarcoid), would reappear or heal over. At the end of the vetting I had to decide; to buy or not to buy. This at the time felt like deciding 'trip or no trip?' A big deep breath and it was game on, hand shake done, Marv was now on the team. I decided to keep Marv at Sunnyside Farm until I could find a livery nearer Edinburgh which was suitable for the training ahead.

The vet volunteered to do the operation herself using a heavy sedative, so a few days later we reconvened at the stable in East Linton. Marv was ready in a loose box with a mountain of straw for protection. He was clearly not happy, he knew something was up and was quite unsettled. The vet tried to administer a dose of anaesthetic but she under estimated the weight (and strength) of Marv. The sedative started to take effect but Marv chose to fight it and battled to stay upright. He was bouncing round the box, banging off the walls like a boxer on his last legs. It was awful to watch and we were powerless to intervene. Finally after 10 minutes of this he did finally collapse. The vet and her assistant went in to try and administer more sedative, but as soon as Marv realised the situation, he started trying to get up again. The operation was embarrassingly aborted. I was not happy, as Marv had been clearly upset, he had managed to obtain many cuts to his head in the process (off the walls), and the lump hadn't been touched. Plan B was to take him to the Royal Dick vet school near Roslin, just south of Edinburgh. A few days later we drove Marv in and I led him into a loose box. This time it went very smoothly. The on-duty vet, with a group of 6 or so vet students came to meet us and we discussed the options. It was decided to use just a local anaesthetic, after a mild sedative. Marv got his mild sedative and I stayed with him at the door of the box while he slowly mellowed. The group came back in 15 minutes and all went into the box. I held Marv's heavy head over the door while they injected a local anaesthetic. 10 minutes later the lump was removed and wound stitched up. If my memory serves me correctly we had Marv back in the box a few hours later, and away

(L) Leading Marv after his operation, (R) the start of the bonding

Marv was now lump free and clearly a solid fighting character. The sad episode of the botched operation showed me an incredibly strong side to Marv's character which would reappear early in the trip. It was now January 2007, and we both had to start our fitness training. One drawback, Marv had just had an operation leaving him with stitches and an inability to wear a saddle for 6 weeks. We could not wait that length of time to start on the miles, so it was bareback time for me. My second ever ride on Marv was at Sunnyside Farm, Marv had been confined to a few weeks box rest and was mad keen to stretch his legs. Fiona and I had managed a walk with Marv round the field a few days back, but we were literally towed round by him. He had energy and wanted to use it. There was no way I wanted to do another walk with him, as I could barely hold him. We didn't know each other yet and he had been through some stressful times and needed to de-stress. When I jumped on Marv with no saddle and walked him out of the yard he was bouncing around like an excited dressage horse. It was all I could do to get him to the field in a jog trot, before he exploded into a fast canter putting in bucks for good measure. I managed to sit tight, grab a handful of mane and kick him on round the field. Luckily his fitness didn't match his enthusiasm and control was regained. Marv had tried to throw me but didn't succeed. That was the last buck Marv ever put in (with me).

Fiona and I researched all the possible livery yards in the Gorebridge area before deciding on a yard called Mountskip (which was run by Sue). I paid extra for full livery and some exercise, as Marv needed to build up the miles while I was still at work during the week. We would visit at weekends and progressively increase the miles up to the planned 20 miles a day distance.

(L & R) Out in rural Midlothian on our training rides with Fi

With the physical training of Marv and myself ongoing, I had still to conclude planning of the trip and this was to include equipment and the route detail. On the equipment front, I was advised by Viv to use a customised saddlebag maker from Cumbria. I contacted the lady and discussed the dimensions of the front and rear saddle bags and the measurements of Marv's back. After putting the order in the saddle bags were made (in 'airborne' maroon of course) and delivered only a few weeks thereafter.

The most important piece of equipment was going to be the saddle. Marv came with a treeless saddle, which I felt would be unsuitable for the trip. That went straight on Ebay. When in the King's Troop I was impressed with the design of the military saddle as so very few horses had any back complaints, despite all using the same saddle. I found out that a company still uses the military basis for making saddles. Free 'N Easy is based in North England and owner Les was very knowledgeable about long distance riding and saddle making. I ordered a new Free 'N Easy saddle for Marv, and the local agent came to the yard to custom fit the saddle. I cannot stress enough how good these saddles are. They have an adjustable flexible plastic pad system, which allows for an exact fit to be made to each horse, and also is able to be adjusted by the rider if and when the horses back muscles change with fluctuating fitness levels.

With my Army training, I had decided right from the off that the trip needed a proper name. All military training exercises were named with something apt. To me this was an exercise as it required planning, specialist training and then execution. I chose Exercise 'Long Trot'. Henceforth the trip would be referred to as such in my planning.

In my initial concept for undertaking the trip I did not envisage raising money for charity, but soon after making the plans for my trip known, friends and family suggested that I should do so.

I chose two charities: the International League for the Protection of Horses (ILPH), who are now called World Horse Welfare, and Cancer Research (for people who were not so keen on horses).

I contacted both charities to let them know of my plan to raise money for them. Cancer Research accepted the application to raise money for them and sent a t-shirt. They recommended opening a Just Giving account. I followed their advice and started a fundraising page.

The ILPH were very excited about the prospect of the trip, as it was directly relevant to their charity, but they had to be sure that my expedition would not contravene their strategy of protecting horses. I essentially had to show them that the trip would not contravene Marv's health, so that the ILPH could actively support it. This I achieved by planning a sensible time to complete the distance, targeting an average of 20 miles a day with a minimum of every Sunday off. I would also be walking (leading Marv) daily if we were not trotting or cantering. It was standard military cavalry procedure up to the 20th century, to preserve the health of the horses by soldiers regularly dismounting and walking with their horses for a period during long marches. Riding a horse in walk is no faster than walking and leading, and walking and leading does help reduce pressure on the horse's body. I perceived that there was no benefit to completing the daily mileage any earlier and so walking and leading a section of each day was an ideal way to maximise the chance of success.

I set up my Just Giving account so that it had an ILPH donation page too. The ILPH helped enormously with putting me into contact with each of their relevant regional officers, who would meet me, see how we were getting on and assist where necessary (for example organising a farrier visit in Staffordshire).

People started donating money as soon as the Just Giving site was open, and so there was no backing down thereafter. Just to be clear, not a single penny of the charitable donations went towards the funding, running or any expense for the trip. I paid for all expenses incurred myself (including horse purchase, stabling during build up training, feed and equipment) and any donations went straight to the charities.

With all the organisation required for the trip, I didn't manage to create a great deal of PR for the trip. Luckily, Ian Fraser (a financial journalist, who lived adjacent to the stables next to Mountskip) did do a fantastic piece in the Scotsman for us. The ILPH ran some great stories on their website and also some local press coverage gained in a few of the areas I travelled through. This relatively small PR coverage meant that the majority of the donations came from people who knew me: friends; family; work colleagues and people who I met on my travels who, once I had met them and explained my trip, gave donations to me to put into Just Giving (in their name).

My sister (a Sgt in the MET police) managed to organise the largest single donation (many £000's) by running a hugely successful charity slave auction at work, including many senior MET officers. Many thanks Sarah.

Early on we decided that a website would be a great way of monitoring progress, both for the build-up training and the trip itself. My friend Mark bravely took on the challenge of the website design and development. I did not realise until afterwards what an onerous task this entailed, as Mark devoted a huge amount of his time, first with me in designing the website and then latterly once the trip started, feeding in the weekly diary updates and photos.

Other bits of kit I ordered for the trip were: a midge net for the north of Scotland; a rubber overshoe in case of a dropped shoe; an equine medical kit and a minimalistic plastic racing bridle which needed little in the way of maintenance.

I had bought the local area 1:25,000 OS maps covering Gorebridge and its surrounding area, and we used these to plan our training. Every weekend Fiona, Maisie (the Parson Russell terrier) and I would drive out to the yard and head off on various planned routes of increasing mileages. As mentioned earlier, the first few weeks of this training involved riding Marv with no saddle as his stitches were still healing. I developed a very good seat and it was comforting knowing I could ride Marv for several hours without stirrups and with no incident. We luckily had the loan of another horse, which Fi rode to keep me company. We would plan the route to include a lunch stop, with a final goal of managing to complete a weekend in April of two 20 mile rides back to back. The lunch stops were great fun. We would find a spot of quiet track and rope off the track 20 yards either side, to allow for the horses to graze while we had our picnic. By now we had the saddle bags in action, and I was getting Marv used to them, by slowly increasing the weight inside them. One concern for the trip was the possible need for hard feed for Marv (especially in the far north, where there was little grass and only heather for some sections).

The detailed route planning was done both at home late into the night and also at work during a period of night shifts. This involved meticulously scanning each 1:50,000 map and highlighting a sensible route for each day between already planned daily stopover locations. The main focus was on keeping off main roads, but also avoiding footpaths and hills where possible. Footpaths are footpaths for a reason, as I had discovered in training and later on the trip. They would be designated bridleways if they were suitable for horses, as they likely had either stiles, locked gates, were too narrow, steep, or crossed streams on bridges unsuitable for horses. I knew that the routes I selected didn't have to be rigidly followed, but knowing that there was a planned route for each day meant one less thing to worry about. I didn't plan the detailed route for the last two weeks (keeping a surprise element to the trip), but I knew in which village I would like to stop. To keep tabs on the planned days I made a trip spreadsheet, which captured each day's start location, OS map numbers, miles travelled, finish location, and any accommodation and contact details known. There were many days already planned in terms of accommodation, predominantly in Scotland. The gaps in accommodation made the trip more exciting for me as I would then have to use my initiative each day to source a field.

By the end of April the training was completed, the kit bought, checked and tested. Marv was fit enough and I was confident of success. A few days before the off we held a send-off barbeque at our house in Morningside for friends and family. I had ordered some maroon polo shirts with the 'Long Trot' logo on it for Fi, Mum, Mark and me, and we all wore them for the evening. It was great to see everyone and there was an energetic expectant air about the trip which buoyed me on.

To get to the start point we needed wheels. I asked the lovely Sonya, owner of Sunnyside Farm, where I had bought Marv, if I could borrow her large horse box. The box was quite new and could take 6 horses. Surprisingly, she very kindly agreed.

<u>Day 0 (Travel from Edinburgh to John O'Groats - 281 miles)</u>

The day before the scheduled start we drove over early to the yard in East Linton to collect the loaned horse box for the long drive to the start. I was very nervous and was in a bit a fluster with the pressure of the trip affecting me. Despite the months of planning, I still had many concerns and was just keen to get started. In my anxiety I managed to slightly bump the horsebox coming out of the yard. Luckily I only had dented the pull down steps, but it still felt like a bad omen. Our good friend Mark had very kindly volunteered to drive with Fi and me up to John O' Groats. We headed back to Edinburgh to pick up Marv and the kit. Once we had loaded up Marv we turned north and headed over the Forth Road Bridge (which I hoped to re-cross in a few weeks' time). Mark and I took turns at the wheel, while Maisie took up a reclining position on the dashboard. I knew that reaching the top of Scotland was a long drive from Edinburgh, but in a horsebox it took the full day.

(L) Loading Marv for the drive to the start, (R) Maisie on the lorry's dashboard on the A9

We stopped just north of Aviemore for a leg stretch for Marv. He had a good munch of grass before being reloaded for the last push up the never ending A9. After Tain the road was ever so slow with so many corners and it followed the coastline like a roller coaster. We began to get large tailbacks behind the lorry, and so we frequently pulled in to relieve the stress of the other motorists. Finally, as we neared the signs for Wick we turned left heading inland off the A9, to facilitate the prepositioning of some (pre bagged) hard horse feed for the first day's stop over at Mybster. We then reached the north coast of Scotland which looked particularly bleak and barren. In my quest to find a stable for Marv for the night, I had been very fortunate in being offered a complimentary night's B&B for Fi and me, and a lovely stable for Marv. Mark offered to spend the night in the horse box snuggled up with the restless Maisie. When we arrived at the farmstead and were being shown the stable for Marv, Maisie raced ahead and went after the owner's ducks. She was luckily prevented just in time from causing an embarrassing scene so soon after arrival. Once Marv was bedded down, the three of us headed to a local pub for the 'last supper'. We were all quite subdued, partially from the long tiring drive and also because of the unknown days ahead.

Week 1 (170 miles)

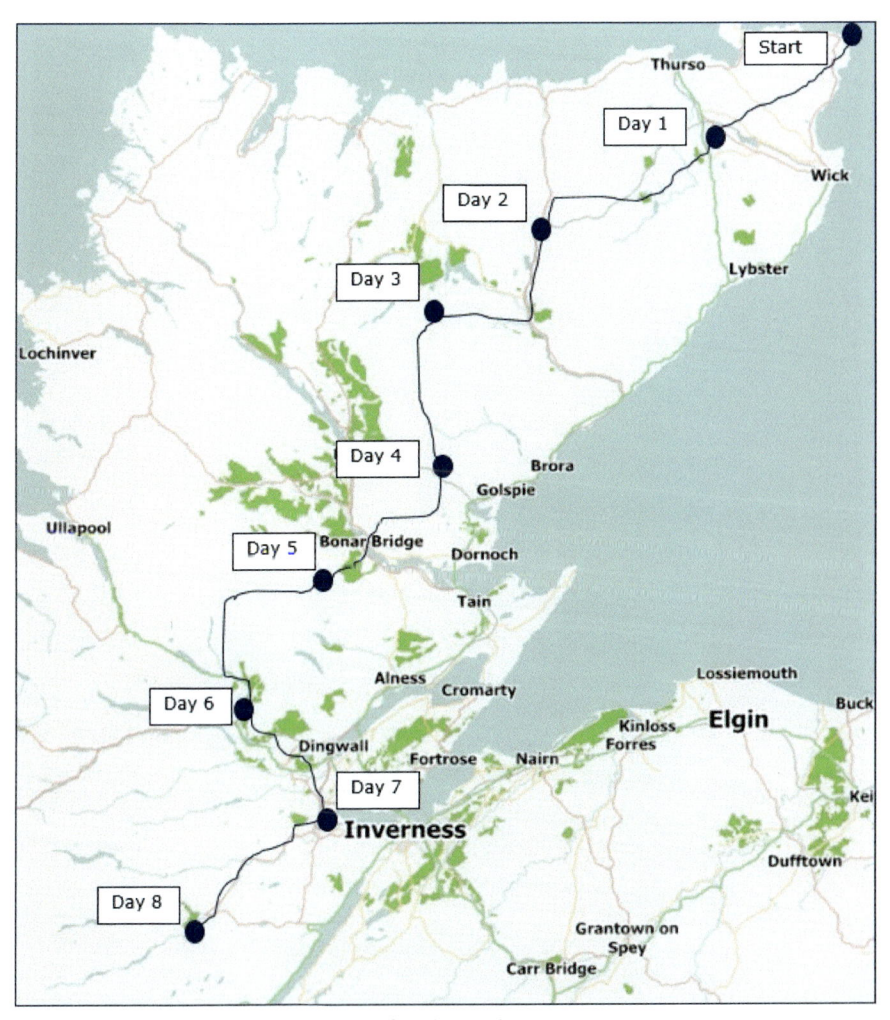

Route showing night stops

Week 1 (total 170 miles – 8 days as start was a Sunday)

<u>Day 1 (John O' Groats to Mybster – 23 miles)</u>

Mark joined us for breakfast in the B&B and soon after it was time to get the show on the road. Marv seemed quite relaxed but alert. The weather was overcast and windy, but at least not raining. We drove the last few miles to John O' Groats and parked the large conspicuous horse box in the deserted car park. There was to be no grand send off today. I was feeling quite nervous and impatient to start on the trip. I knew we had to mark the start with some photographs, so I quickly saddled up Marv and attached the saddle bags and dry bag behind the saddle. Marv was now getting restless as he picked up on my tension. I felt guilty that shortly I was going to leave Fi and Mark behind, as they had spent so much of their time and effort getting me and Marv to the start and on the trip in general. They had to spend the day driving the empty box back to Edinburgh.

(L) Marv looking pensive at John O'Groats, (R) trying to stand still for the start photo

Frustratingly the dry bag would not sit straight behind the saddle. I would somehow have to sort this out later, but I didn't have the patience right now. Photos were taken with the John O' Groats ferry behind and I quickly said my goodbyes. Marv and I rode off southwest and the adventure had officially started. I had only gone 1km before the annoying dry bag had slipped round and was hanging off again. I could see the horse box just leaving the car park so I called Fi and asked if they could drive over. Embarrassingly, I got off and took out a heavy horse blanket from the dry bag and threw it in the horse box. Far more relaxed as the kit now sat better, we said our goodbyes again and this time they drove off and I started the long slog south.

The first day's mileage was a reasonable amount. Strategically I had planned to try and be in Aberfeldy (near Pitlochry) by the second weekend to ensure we got some days off and this could coincide with Fi being able to join us. To achieve this goal we had to manage some long mileage days in the first fortnight.

The next day was fairly straightforward. Marv kept looking round to where we had come from in a slightly mournful and longing way. There was not much to see as the land is quite flat and featureless in the north east corner of Scotland. We made good time and reached the first night's destination by 1600. We were both tired as much emotionally as physically. First thing was to pick up the hard feed drop we had prepositioned the day before. Next was to get a field or stable sorted for Marv. I had nothing booked for night one. The location I had picked was just a small hamlet on the map. I asked at a bungalow which had fields attached, and the friendly occupant not only offered Marv a field, but also offered a bed for me. Result! We turned Marv out and he got his hard feed for the day. I was carrying several kilos worth of Dodson & Horrell Staypower muesli mix in freezer bags, but these would only last a few days. I could only hope that we could source enough food (grass) en route for him. I carried a small stove, some noodles, muesli and dried milk, which could also sustain me for a few days. Re-provisioning for both of us would be something I needed to think about daily.

Day 2 (Mybster to Fosinard – 23 miles)

After an overcast and unremarkable first day, we were rewarded with a bright sunny outlook on day two. I welcomed the proffered cooked breakfast and then packed up my gear to go and see how Marv was. It seemed he had already made friends with the owner's Clydesdale mare and was not too keen to be saddled up to head off. We bade farewell and headed southwest towards the Fosinard Hotel. The scenery was particularly spectacular as we passed a large wind farm to our left on the horizon. The road ended abruptly at Westerdale and we then followed landrover tracks across increasingly heathery terrain. I was beginning to be concerned that there might not be enough grazing for Marv in the next few days, and also a lack of fencing to prevent him wandering off.

Still quite nervous with regard to our daily routine, I stopped for lunch on the shore of Loch More. There was plenty of grass by the bank and I decided that I would try to let Marv have an hour without his saddle. To facilitate this I clipped him onto a long lightweight lunge line and sat down for a breather whilst he happily munched away. After a very pleasant hour I packed up and tried to re-saddle Marv. Instantly I realised there was a fundamental problem that there was nowhere to tie him up to. Predictably he wouldn't stand still, and it took me 30 minutes to wrestle on the saddle and saddle bags whilst spinning in a circle. This lunchtime experiment was not to be repeated, but we were starting to learn what worked and what didn't. Nevertheless, slightly flustered we headed off past the remote Altnabreac railway station, across country and through forestry blocks making good progress. Marv discovered puddle slurping. As well as my general concern for grazing, I carried a collapsible water carrier. We had tried in training to get Marv to drink from this, but to no avail. Today saw him drink his fill from any number of the muddy puddles we passed. I thereafter knew he would be fine for water consumption and ditched the water carrier after the first week. We managed many long trots on the tracks, alternating with me walking with Marv. Finally, we dropped down onto the A897 single track road and completed the last few miles to see the welcome sight of the remote hotel. I had prearranged a field for Marv with the owners. Once introduced to the landlord, I found Marv his field and put up my bivi for the night. I had my first night's meal cooked by stove, a nutritious noodle and tuna mix. After supper I headed into the pub for a relaxing pint. In the bar there was only me, two contractors (who were working on the overhead pylons) and a gentleman eating on his own. The two contractors and I shared a few jars, and just as I got up to go, they very generously gave a £50 donation towards the charities I was raising money for. My first night in the bivi was very comfortable, lying on long soft grass under my sleeping bag and having completed two longish days, I was soon asleep dreaming of the days to come.

Day 3 (Fosinard to Gearnsay – 19 miles)

We were up early and off south on another bright blue sky day. We had a few miles to do on the quiet A897 (single track A road) before heading west across country again. I was now relaxing into the trip and Marv was settling nicely too. He still looked round for the first few miles every morning as if to check the location of his last field in case he needed to return. It was only half an hour after departure when I was overtaken by a small convertible car and the chap at the wheel introduced himself as the 'other' man in the bar last night. It turned out he was a freelance reporter for Radio Scotland and was up north working. Would I mind being interviewed? "Not at all", I said, "as long as we could do it on the move". I was keen not to lose any time. He then parked up and walked alongside us for 15 minutes whilst we chatted away into his Dictaphone. He said farewell and I carried on. Apparently the piece did go out on air soon after, as my uncle heard the interview one morning.

(L) & (R) Fantastic views of Loch Badenloch

After Kinbrace we headed west on the B871 and then turned off onto tracks heading towards Ben Klibreck. We stopped for lunch at Loch Badanloch which had a glorious sandy beach and postcard views all around. I had made no plans for this night's stop as there was no settlement anywhere near the 20 mile marker, and so I was concerned as to where we would spend the night. I had seen a bothy on the OS map and decided that this was to be the place. We reached the bothy mid-afternoon and my fears were realised as there were no fences to be seen. There were the remains of a stone wall surrounding some short grass on one side of the bothy, which was a start. The local ghillie came up on his quad later on as he had heard that I was planning on passing through the area. He luckily allowed Marv to eat some of his deer feed (sugar beet pellets) which he had stored in the bothy. For the first 2 hours I tied up Marv to the one tree and set about rebuilding as much of the wall enclosure as I could, by moving stones and using lengths of para cord to help secure the gaps. It certainly wouldn't stop a determined escape attempt and if Marv got out he had thousands of acres of heather to explore with no fences to stop him. As the weather was still warm, I stripped off and went down to the nearby clear mountain stream for a proper wash in the clear cool water. The next 24 hours were to be my most memorable of the trip.

(L) & (R) The makeshift enclosure at the bothy

You could see no other settlements or signs of life from the bothy and the views were spectacular. A herd of deer came over to have a look at what we were doing. Marv instantly spotted them and was transfixed. I thought that he might jump out and join them at any minute. As it was a clear night, I risked not putting the poncho up and just used the bivi bag option. I decided to sleep across one of the gaps in the wall so I could at least keep an eye on Marv during the night. Once in my sleeping bag sleep proved difficult and I kept waking periodically to see if he was still there, until about midnight when I finally fell asleep.

Day 4 (Gearnsay to Rogart – 21 miles)

At dawn, I woke up and cautiously looked out of my sleeping bag over into the homemade enclosure adjacent to me to check that Marv was still there. Yes he was! He was still asleep, and he was lying down right next to me. I was quite touched by this and managed to get a few photos before we both got up.

(L) Waking up to Marv next to me, (R) heading up the side of Ben Armine

Feeling revitalised after managing the memorable night by the bothy, we struck off south heading for Ben Armine Lodge, as the Loch Choire route was deemed to be too boggy by the locals. We faced a strong climb as we rounded the side of Ben Armine, but were making good progress on this long day. We were following a quite distinct and well used track when we came across a fairly nondescript stream. I was on foot at this point, but Marv continued to refuse to cross the stream. We had to get over the other side and continue on our path, so I decided to lead him 20 metres to the left where the crossing seemed easier. We both got across ok and were heading back to rejoin the path when Marv almost immediately sank down to his belly in a peat bog.

Oh fXXX! Disaster. Marv became instantly distressed and tried using brute force to get out, to no avail. I got the saddle and bags off and dumped them back on the path. I clipped on the lunge line to his head collar and tried to take stock of the situation. We were miles from anywhere, there was no mobile signal. I had a 'heavy horse' now stuck in peat bog and trying in vain to extricate himself. Then noises coming from his legs as he thrashed around suggested that he may have broken or torn something already, which could be the end of Marv (if he needed to be put down as a consequence). It was fair to say that I shed some tears and cursed myself continually as I dug around his front legs with my hands to aid him getting his feet clear. He was sweated up all over and working very hard to get out. We slowly established a routine, whereby once I had dug out his front feet sufficiently and he had got his breathing back, he then managed to haul himself a metre closer to the track with me pulling on the lunge line. This process was repeated over and over for an hour until he finally pulled himself clear of the peat bog. He stood back on the path and shook himself all over, whilst I couldn't believe he had done it. I had visions of him having broken his leg or having to be pulled out by a helicopter.

We both got a huge shock and were visibly traumatised. But having got through this event together, I believe it bonded us in such a strong way that from then on we both trusted each other on a whole new level. Marv stood quite still while I saddled him up. There were no indications of a break or tear to his legs. We moved off, now back on the track, so glad that the incident had had a happy ending. My mind was a muddle for hours afterwards, and huge lessons were learnt. We were both physically and emotionally tired and we still had many miles to go. After passing Ben Armine Lodge we were both so glad to be walking on tarmac again. My awareness of suitable terrain for horse movement was heightened and I vowed to always take the sensible route from here on in.

We slogged on and reached the outskirts of Rogart. As we started passing the first few cottages there was a lady outside her front door cleaning a saddle and drinking wine. We stopped and got chatting to Kosie who insisted that she could find a stable for Marv in the village. She gave directions to Rovie Farm, as she knew the local farmer John. Sure enough when we reached Rovie we were met by John and Marv had a deep straw bed ready in a stabled open barn amongst John's own horses. Marv got a huge feed from John and enjoyed a good night's rest. John also invited me to stay in the farmhouse, which was very generous. Weirdly, somehow in the short space of time I had been there, John had managed to track down my mother's cousin who happened to live locally and she appeared with her guitar playing man friend for a surreal gathering. I was far too tired for this, and after a whisky and a short round of conversation, I excused myself to bed.

Day 5 (Rogart to Amat – 24 miles)

Having survived the drama of yesterday I was looking forward to getting our collective confidence back and having a simpler day. Again, the weather was favourable and I looked at my planned route which started by heading up a steep deforested side of a mountain. There was no real route for the first few miles, as I had planned on using some forestry tracks which I thought would get me over to a single track south of Rogart. John agreed that the route was not obvious or easy but was achievable. After leaving Rovie Farm I headed south looking for the track on my map. There was no sign of it to be found. With no real alternative (and acutely aware of yesterday's incident) I was forced to lead Marv up a steep section of ground, which I struggled to climb. Marv also struggled with his footing in places, as this was mountain goat territory and not suitable for Clydesdales. Marv mistakenly trod on me during the ascent and ripped off one of my half chaps in our mad scramble. Once we had reached the summit, we found a path of sorts, but it ran east / west. We needed to go south. I then took a bearing and headed off across the heather to find the road. We were both nervous as yesterday's lesson was fresh in our minds. Marv was super cautious and if he was in any doubt as to the firmness of the ground he would stop and sniff for peat. I also scanned ahead looking for the best ground. It was slow progress and I was convinced that off-roading with Marv was not suitable in the Highlands. We finally found the road two hours after leaving Rovie which was a very slow way to cover three miles on one of the longest days. However once on the tarmac we made up good time with long spells of trot (some of which I chose to run to give Marv a break).

(L) Bonar Bridge lunch stop, (R) bivi in Glen Carron

We made Bonar Bridge by late lunch and a welcome stop at the Spar. I had a nose bleed in the Spar which was unusual, and Marv got his carrots/apple snack whilst I refuelled. We took a great photo of us with the (Arnhem type) bridge behind us and amazingly still blue sky. The afternoon's miles were to be heading west up the road on the south side of Glen Carron. I marvelled at the spectacular scenery around us, with great views of the adjacent river with its salmon pools and numerous estate houses and cottages. Again, we managed a good average speed by achieving many trots and runs. As we neared Amat we stopped at a bungalow, and Katie the owner kindly provided Marv with a bucket of water. I enquired about a field for Marv and she kindly said we could use her field located a few miles up the Glen. She also noted that her farrier was coming to attend her horse tomorrow morning, and could possibly look at Marv's shoes. This was very useful and timely as one shoe was starting to become loose. I duly noted the directions to the field and we headed off up the glen. The field was perfect for us. It had a water standpipe over an old bath which Marv could use for a drink and had great views. I pitched the poncho onto the fence line and did some washing. It was a perfect evening and we could both relax somewhat having regained some composure from the last two days' exertions. It was nice to have only Marv for company for the night in the field. As I was sleeping in the same field as Marv, once in my sleeping bag, he came over and sniffed my head to check up on me and to see if I had any snacks. I did worry that he might inadvertently step on me through the poncho, or catch his feet on my bungees and run off with my shelter in the night. I felt I was starting to get the rhythm of the trip with five of the hardest days (in terms of remoteness and distance) under our belts. I fell asleep very contented and proud of Marv.

Day 6 (Amat to Inchbae Lodge – 20 miles)

The local farrier stopped off early to put some more nails into one of Marv's shoes and I realised that he would need a new set of shoes in Aberfeldy in a week's time. Somehow I had started the trip with one set of new rear shoes and a set of front shoes that were 2 weeks old. This was for a good reason as Marv didn't have great hoof. By keeping on a set of newish front shoes meant that the hoof wall would retain some strength as new nail holes frequently meant cracking. This meant that the front and rears needing shoeing alternately and so twice as many farrier visits. In hindsight I would not recommend shoeing in pairs. Although as the rear shoes were wearing faster it may be that it was always going to be split shoeing.

It was going to be a remote day today, with no settlements or shops on the route. We were to go up Glen More and pass Deanich Lodge into Strath Vaich. Straight away I started to find issues with cattle grids where deer fences met the road. We would sometimes find no gate alongside the cattle grid, or the gate was locked. I carried a big set of fencing pliers which I used on the odd occasion to allow for temporary access requirements. The track wound past Alladale Lodge, and Marv stopped to say hello to some grey ponies (used for deer stalking) who were pleased to see a fellow equine. Alladale was experimenting with wild boar enclosures and we passed many signs warning us of the dangers they may present. None were spotted, but I daresay that if Marv had spotted any, our average speed would have been quicker! Traversing this long glen surrounded on both sides by 2000ft mountains was inspiring. It was this day when I think that Marv realised what the trip was all about - "20 miles south each day and no going back". For the first few days I experimented with letting him loose when I was walking with him, but he often stopped and turned around and started heading north. Today when I tried it, he somehow just knew we had to keep on going. We would often walk for miles side by side with his reins tucked up into his head collar. If I stopped for a pee, he would just carry on walking and I would catch him up. This made me feel confident in that we both now knew what we had to do.

(L) Meeting the Alladale ponies, (R) stunning Strath Vaich

Around midday, we reached a lodge where three glens meet. There were people staying there and we got chatting. This was a guest shooting lodge for the Alladale Estate (coincidentally where a friend of mine, Barclay, ended up working a few years later). They were very generous to us and shared their packed lunches which meant many apples for Marv. Into the afternoon we were still making good progress as we passed Loch Vaich and headed down the Hydro Electric track to the A835. Today was exciting as Fi and Maisie were heading north to see us and would meet us at Inchbae Lodge.

(L) Maisie and Marv share a carrot, (R) camping at Inchbae

The Grants (no relation) farmed at Inchbae, and provided us with a lush field through which flowed a clear stream. After ensuring Marv was ok, I was offered the luxury of a superb shower and to join the family for their evening meal. Fi was still en route north so after supper I offered to go with Sandy Grant to check on the sheep. When we got back Fi and 'the mooch' (Maisie's nickname) had arrived and it was fantastic to see them. We put up the tent Fi had brought and I recounted the first week's adventures. Marv also did well as Fi had brought a bag of Dodson & Horrell mix to keep his strength up. Maisie enjoyed the mix too and so the little and large animals were munching side by side out of the same feed bucket.

Day 7 (Inchbae Lodge to Muir of Ord – 19 miles)

Fi had brought some great food with her in a cool box and we had a tasty camper's breakfast before packing up. It was now Saturday and we were due to meet my Mother and Ken for lunch at Contin. I left with Marv taking Maisie for extra company, and headed off alongside Loch Garve through some stunning woodland tracks. Maisie loved the exercise and the tracks were great under foot, so we managed several miles of canter. Marv enjoyed the variety of going faster on good ground and stretching his muscles. We arrived at the hotel and managed to persuade the hotel owner to allow Marv to graze the adjacent field, which had nice long grass. It was great to see Mum and Ken too and to share with them the news of week one. During lunch Maisie got stung in the eye by a bumble bee whilst outside on the patio, so she then looked like a boxer with one eye closed.

(L) & (R) Heading for Contin through the forest

Having had a pint for lunch, it was hard to get back on the road and do the last miles to Muir of Ord. Mum, Ken and Fi all left by car and I headed off with Marv to do the last half of the day. Marv and I plodded on crossing the River Conon and passing through Marybank on the A832. 'The team' had helped us out by scouting ahead and securing a stable for Marv at Chapelton Farm equestrian centre. When we arrived at the yard, in the next door stable to Marv was a sick horse which was very unwell. Its owners were doing a sitting vigil in the barn as we left Marv for the night. There was nothing that anybody could do to help, the vet had been and it was a question of time. Mum and Ken had generously booked Fi and me into the local hotel for a proper bed (and my first bath). The long soak was restorative and morale boosting. I sorted all my kit in the hotel room, ditching the fly rug, as I had only used it once, and it was very heavy. After a great pub meal I got an early night as there was to be no rest day tomorrow, that was still a week away.

Day 8 (Muir of Ord to Tomich – 21 miles)

We had a superb 'full Scottish' breakfast, then checked out to head down to see Marv at the local yard. The sad news was that Marv's neighbour had not lasted the night and we were greeted with an empty stable upon arrival. So it was with quiet contemplation that I saddled up Marv and headed out on the road for day eight. Today started dry, but turned out to be the wettest on the trip. Soon after Beauly, I pulled on the waterproofs and we kept plodding on southwest. I had Maisie for company for a few miles, but as the rain started she opted for the car quite sensibly. As it was a Sunday my weekend visitors would be leaving mid-afternoon, and the knowledge of this added to my slightly dampened spirits. Uncle Douglas and Aunt Joan had driven across from Lossiemouth today to say hello, and they caught up with me on the road up Strath Glass. They then all went off for a pub lunch at Struy leaving Marv and me to continue the miles. At the pub they had bought and warmed some red wine which was duly produced in a screw top bottle and made me look like a wandering wino. The wine helped morale and it was good to catch up with them albeit only for a few minutes in the rain.

(L) & (C) Tired and wet in Strath Glass, (R) in the barn at Tomich

Once my family had left, the day thereafter was just head down and onwards. When we arrived much later in Tomich, I got some poor directions off a local and wasted 90 minutes going up the wrong track. At 1900 I finally found the barn which I had previously organised. The open barn had no sides but was half full of large round hay bales. This would have to do. I tied up a para cord round the barn columns to make a temporary fence for Marv. He then had unlimited hay on tap. I found a bucket and water for Marv and could then set about my dinner of noodles. I slept on top of the round bales whilst Marv happily munched the hay all around me. Although I arrived tired and a bit annoyed from the wasted time at the end of the day, it was a most memorable night in the barn.

Week 2 (85 miles)

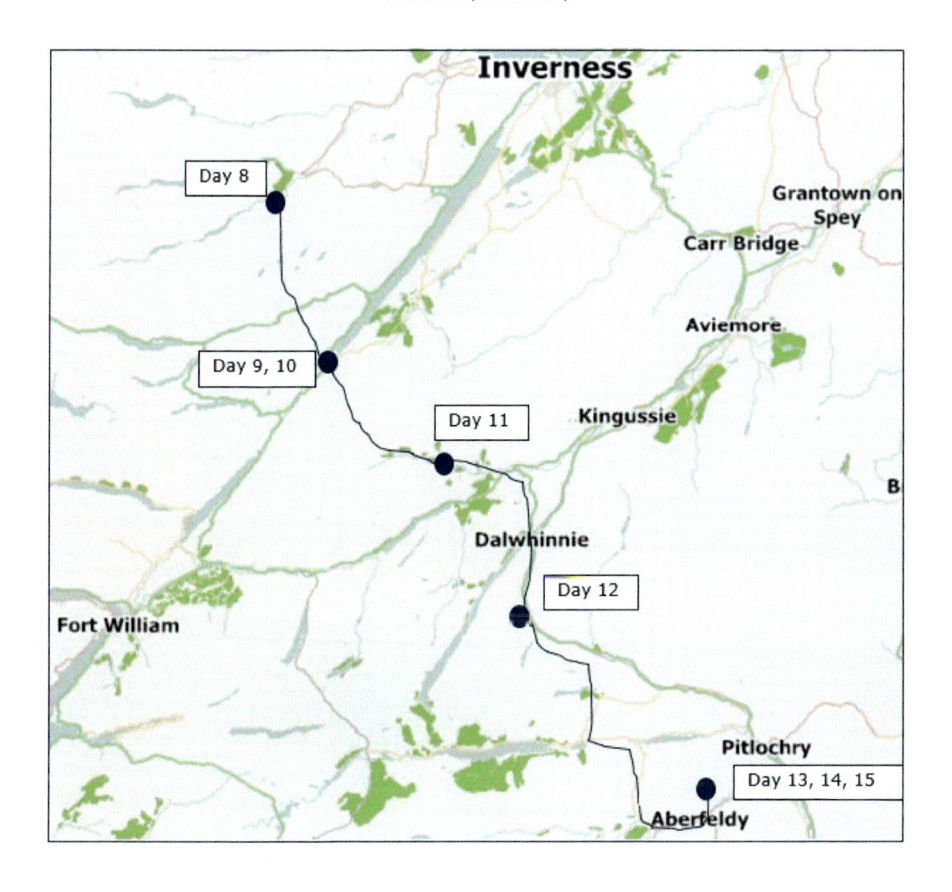

Week 2 (total 85 miles)

Day 9 (Tomich to Fort Augustus – 16 miles)

Today was due to be a little shorter in length, being less than 20 miles, but it was to be quite a bleak heather-strewn landscape with no settlements on route. There were also two big climbs to take in. The land rover track followed a pylon line for a while and we were making good progress for the first few hours into a strong headwind. I happened to look back at Marv and noticed that my camouflage rucksack cover (which I was using as a saddle cover) was missing. Bitterly disappointed that it was gone, instead of just accepting the fact, I made the fatal mistake of assuming it had only just blown off and that I could find it. I was so annoyed at myself I actually said to Marv "stay here mate, I'll be back in a minute". I then proceeded to run back down the track on the lookout for the lost item. Marv was not keen on staying put and started trotting to follow me. I finally gave up after half an hour of fruitless running and the back track of two miles. As I turned round, Marv stared at me indignantly suggesting 'what the hell was that all for?' I was so embarrassed, to then have to go back over the same two miles again unnecessarily. Adding four miles to the day was just stupid and I needed to get real. As well as losing the saddle cover I also lost a small bag with tent pegs and other essential items which had fallen out as Marv had cantered over the heather in pursuit of me. My military training had clearly faded and some more self-discipline was needed fast. On the plus side, Marv was getting much braver and was seen to be fording a two foot deep river, having earlier in trip shied at a shallow stream.

Just before losing my saddle cover

We arrived in Fort Augustus later in the day to find a hugely welcoming Mrs Findlay at her small holding on the outskirts of the village. Marv's rear shoes were not in good shape and the pair were looking loose and worn. I managed to call Robin Pape, the local farrier, and he said he could attend to Marv, but not until later the next day. It would mean losing a day of the schedule, which I really didn't want to do, but the steep Corrieyairack Pass was the next section, and this would be hard on Marv's feet. If he lost a shoe on this section, it could put the trip in jeopardy. Mrs Findlay very kindly allowed me to stay an extra day and night to wait for the farrier. In fairness, Marv and I both badly needed the rest day anyway. We had pushed so hard since the start with long miles completed each day, that this set back was actually a positive. Mrs Findlay's home cooking was excellent and I met her son who ran a small sawmill on the property.

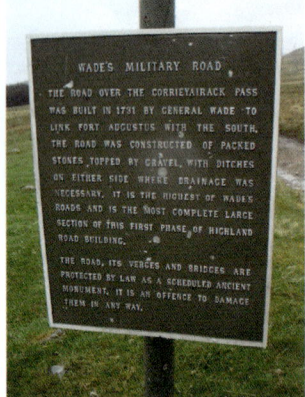

(L) Marv samples verge at Fort Augustus, (R) Wade's road out of Fort Augustus

Day 10 (Fort Augustus – enforced rest day)

A day of bliss for us, but Marv had on his midge hood as there were a few of the beasties around. He shared his field with some chickens and sheep and did very well for some extra snacks. I wandered into Fort Augustus to send Fi a postcard and top up on supplies. During the day I managed to read a book on the construction of the Caledonian Canal which was built by renowned civil engineer Thomas Telford. I thought this book was particularly apt as Fort Augustus was located midway on the canal and had a series of locks which took years to build. It was good to learn a bit of local history whilst passing through. My shins were giving me a bit of grief and also the arch on my left foot was sore. This day helped relieve these pressures a little. Marv was still sound and was looking in great shape. He had lost some weight, but his muscle definition was excellent. I had become aware that if the saddle bags were not secured correctly saddle rubs occurred, and so I managed to invent a system which prevented any future rubs. Arriving mid-afternoon, Robin was a great bearded bear of a man with a superb character. He sorted Marv out with a new set of rear shoes which would hold sound for many miles. We were now all set to proceed on the trip first thing next morning.

(L) Robin changes rear shoes, Marv has his midge head net on, (R) Marv's mates

Day 11 (Fort Augustus – Laggan – 18 miles)

Mrs Findlay cooked another superb breakfast and sent me on my way with a comprehensive packed lunch. So with a much more relaxed peace of mind and rested bodies we headed off for the Corrieyairack Pass. This was one of General Wade's military roads and the pass climbed to 760 metres. The weather was fair and the views fantastic. As we had the benefit of the break I think we both enjoyed the day much more. It wasn't the slog it had been a few days ago.

(L) & (R) Up and over the pass

When we reached the top of the pass we looked southeast towards Dalwhinnie and the A9, which we would be reaching tomorrow. Half way down the pass I was met by Fred, who had canoed in the RAF with my father. He walked with us down to Laggan and took some photos and a short video of Marv walking across a bridge on his own whilst following us. We stopped at Garvamore where we met Duncan and Pete who had made a field available for Marv. I put my bivi up in the field and gratefully joined the family for dinner. They wouldn't allow me to sleep outside, so I quickly accepted the offer of the sofa.

(L) & (R) Down the pass and back onto roads

Day 12 (Laggan to Dalnaspidal Lodge – 21 miles)

In the morning, Pete's wife Lisa and daughter Jessica managed to see Marv before she left for school. Marv had made overnight friends with a black mare, and made numerous neighing calls as we departed. I had organised to meet up with Jim the local International League for the Protection of Horses (ILPH) field officer, near Catlodge. He had brought coffee and sandwiches for us and we chatted away whilst Marv happily grazed outside a visitor centre. We talked about the trip and it was good to know that the ILPH were being very supportive of us. I was keen to ensure that their faith in me was not misplaced. After Jim had left, Marv and I made good time and reached Dalwhinnie by lunch time. I had planned to stop here, and had organised a stable for Marv.

Pausing for a quick munch just north of Dalwhinnie

I found the stable, took the saddle off Marv and put him in, and enjoyed my sandwiches whilst contemplating my options. On my original planned route I had added an extra loop to go up to Kingussie and down Glen Tromie. This was because it looked a scenic route to take. But as I had lost a day due to Marv's shoes, I saw an opportunity to claw back the day and get back on schedule. This was important, as I had many nights planned to stay with people and I didn't want to be ringing everyone to change the days. Also the weekends were planned to coincide with being at certain places so I could share my day off with people. By cutting out this extra leg (the route would have taken me northeast for a few miles) I could still make Aberfeldy for the weekend. So I made the decision to push on south down the A9 today to see how far I could get. Marv thought that the walking was over for the day and was getting comfortable in the stable. I saddled him back up and pushed on. This was Thursday and Fi was heading north to meet me after work.

Once we reached the A9, there is a footpath/cyclepath adjacent to the very busy road, but quite often the path is only one metre away from the carriageway. Marv is bulletproof and was not fussed at all by the speeding traffic. We got numerous positive beeps on the horn from passing motorists which kept the spirits up. After Dalwhinnie there are no more settlements until Bruar, only a few hunting lodges. I began to wonder where I might put Marv for the night. There were no fields or fences to be seen, only open heather moorland. I tried the solitary B&B on the way to Drumochter, but they were full and not too helpful. My goal was Dalnacardoch Lodge just short of Bruar, where we were scheduled to stay, but I doubted if we would make it that far. In the end we made it to Dalnaspidal Lodge just before dark and the local landowner allowed Marv a sheltered field just off the A9. I put my bivi up just in time to take shelter from a hail storm, but Marv had no option but to just brave it out. Fi and Maisie arrived soon after with bags of morale. We put a rug on Marv and the mooch (Maisie's nickname) kept Marv company during his dinner of Dodson & Horrell mix, while Fi and I put up the tent for a night of relative comfort. The incredibly well organised Fi had again produced a sumptuous picnic dinner from a cool box overflowing with tasty treats. I was glad to be through the Drumochter pass of the A9 as this marked the end of the Highlands section of the trip and it was onwards towards Perthshire and Edinburgh, which felt like going home.

(L), (C) & (R) In the field by Dalnaspidal Lodge

Day 13 (Dalnaspidal Lodge to Tirnie Farm – 25 miles)

As we had not quite reached our original intended destination for day 12, we now had extra miles to do today to get back on schedule. It was an early start for us all. Marv came to say hello by sticking his big head into the tent to say good morning and to see where his breakfast was. He was careful not to stand on the tent with his huge feet, but you could see they were very close to the edge of the fly sheet. Maisie thought this was a great game and jumped on Marv's nose whereby the two animals careered off down the field together.

Hoof pick before start

I doubted whether I would reach Aberfeldy in one day, so the plan was just to do as many miles as was comfortable. I soon passed the lodge where we had been expected the night before and then swung south on the quiet road up and over the moor into Trinafour. I had agreed to meet Fi there around midday. When Fi found me, I was chatting to Bob, who was the Auchleek Estate's gamekeeper (we began chatting as I had cut a corner by crossing his land). He cordially invited Fi and me for lunch in the village with his employer, the local farmer Alec and his wife Martha. We headed down the hill and found the farm house. Marv had a bale of hay to tuck into whilst we had a veritable spread of a lunch inside. After a splendid surprise lunch stop we headed south on the road to Tummel Bridge. We managed a long canter here, the first in a long time, and it was good for us both. Marv enjoyed doing something other than just walk and trot. However, the hills were still plentiful and the gradients slowed the average speed. I sent Fi off on a mission to find a field this side of Aberfeldy as we were not going to make the full distance today. We ploughed on and then got the call that she had located a suitable field from a local farmer. When Marv and I finally caught up with Fi having done 25 miles, we were gratefully shown the field and we left a relieved Marv with his dinner for the night. It felt weird to be leaving Marv on his own for the first time, but he was not bothered, just glad of the grass and a rest. We headed down to our cottage for the weekend near Aberfeldy and I had a long soak in the bath. It was great to have made it to the end of week 2 (nearly) and a lot of self-imposed pressure about our ability to complete the trip was dissipating, now we were in Perthshire.

(L) & (R) Relaxing in the cottage near Aberfeldy

Day 14 (Tirnie Farm to Aberfeldy – 5 miles, nearly a rest day)

Feeling very relaxed, but a bit stiff in the legs, we drove back the 5 miles to Marv's field. There he was, all alert and waiting by the gate for the next leg. He was not to know it was only a short stint today. To give him a bigger break, we went without a saddle, and I alternately rode him bareback and walked him the short distance to our weekend lodgings near Aberfeldy. Mooch joined us once we turned off the main road. We got Marv up to the cottage by mid-morning on the Saturday, and we had thereby earned an almost full rest day. I sorted out my saddle and equipment, doing some repairs and some repacking of kit. It was just good to spend time with Fi and the Mooch and not be on the move for once. Both Marv and I ate very well at Aberfeldy and we were very well looked after. I changed from my Jodhpur boots to trainers as the arch on my left foot was still giving me grief. It was made worse, by continually mounting Marv several times a day, and the ensuing twisting action in my foot getting into the saddle's stirrups. The trainers helped, but I still had no idea what the issue was.

Marv says hello

Day 15 (Aberfeldy rest day)

This was a purely luxurious day which lifted my spirits. I spent some time going over the detail of the trip so far with Fi. We also spent time with Marv ensuring he was ok and had no niggles. I adjusted the saddle to fit Marv's changing shape, as he was now becoming more athletic and his back muscles had developed further. It was great to catch up with the Mooch, who thought the trip was good fun and couldn't see why she couldn't do the whole thing. I did suggest it to Fi who said that losing both me and Marv for a few months was bad enough. A fair point, no more discussion needed on the matter.

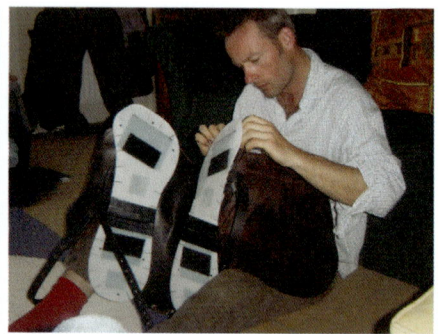

(L) Marv enjoying his first day off, (R) adjusting the saddle to Marv's stronger back

We spent some time going through the diary entries for the 'Long Trot' website, which was a live site before and during the trip. During the trip I made a daily diary entry in my largely illegible scribble. This was done each night after Marv was sorted and I had managed to feed myself. The mission was to get the diary information back to base (ie Fi) and from there onto the website in good time. I tried my best to call Fi daily, if the mobile signal allowed. That allowed her to get a flavour of any news or issues I had. I then either sent the weekly diary entries to her by post, or when I was still in Scotland by hand (as I met up with her for the first three weekends). Fi then had to somehow decode my handwriting, turn it into legible type and get Julian (our academic on the team) to cross check the text, before Mark uploaded it to the website. Together with the text, I also forwarded the week's photos on a memory card. Oblivious to the lengthy process this was, I occasionally became frustrated if the diary was a week behind, forgetting that they still had their jobs to do concurrently. If the trip was done again now, an IPhone would be all that would be required to keep any interested followers updated with text, photos and tweets. Also it would ease the pressure on the backup team.

Week 3 (79 miles)

Week 3 (total 79 miles)

Day 16 (Aberfeldy to Amulree - 11 miles)

To round off a thoroughly pleasant weekend with Fi, our first day of week three was a stroll of 11 miles. I had pre booked a room in the hotel at Amulree, and they had provided a field next to the hotel for Marv. After saying goodbye to Fi and Mooch, we headed through Aberfeldy by crossing the old bridge to the north and then taking the A826 south through Glen Cochill. We had dropped some hard feed at the Hotel over the weekend, so Marv had his 3kg helping waiting for him upon our arrival at lunchtime. It so happened that Rob, a school friend, who was flying helicopters in Florida, was over in the UK and decided to fly north to catch up with me. He borrowed my car from Edinburgh and drove up to see me at Amulree. He picked me up at the Hotel in the afternoon and we drove off to nearby Dunkeld for a coffee and a natter. It was great to see Rob, as he was one of the first people to introduce me to horses. Having an afternoon off with a shorter day coincided nicely with him being in the UK. He dropped me back at the hotel and headed off. I had a dinner for one at the empty hotel and went to bed keeping an eye on Marv from my bedroom window. I started to feel that I had become a bit soft, after having spent nights under the bivi in a field with Marv, I was now in a hotel room. I actually had a bed organised all the way to Edinburgh this week so this was going to be an easy week compared to the first two.

Field adjacent to the Amulree Hotel

Day 17 (Amulree to Clathy - 17 miles)

We both enjoyed a big breakfast today before heading south on the stunning route towards Findo Gask. The first section through the Sma'Glen saw Marv play up a little. We were on the A822, on which there was little traffic, when Marv spotted a tractor coming the other way. I couldn't keep him straight and he wheeled round and cantered off back down the road. I soon got him back to a walk and pulled in to a field to let the tractor go by. I put it down to him being in high spirits and full of beans. There was certainly a new spring in his step today. The verges were getting lusher and there were grassy fields which replaced the Highland heather. Also we were passing many more horses in surrounding fields which raised his equine morale.

(L) Riding through the Sma'Glen, (R) lunch break in same

After turning off the A822, we came into Glenalmond which was stunning and serene. Soon after, on the back roads, we came across a carrot on the road. I picked it up and fed it to Marv. A few metres on, we found another carrot. I thought that someone was planting these for us. However, the carrot trail grew bigger and soon it was numerous carrots all over the road. How strange! We passed a farm where there was the biggest mound of carrots and parsnips piled up like an orange snow drift. Marv was not happy. This was unusual to him and must have posed a threat, as he started walking away sideways keeping a look out for the scary orange pile which might attack at any moment. I couldn't believe he didn't want to dive in and gorge himself on vegetables.

(L) Carrot mountain, (R) quick break on the quiet lanes

Later on, at Clathy we found the house of a friend of Mum and Ken. John and Helen had a paddock at the end of their garden, which Marv immediately made his home. I attempted to hose down Marv to give him a good clean, but Marv hopped around on his lead rope and made the process difficult. Later, I was gratefully taken to the characterful local pub at Dunning for a drink after an evening meal of homemade lasagne (three portions!) and rhubarb crumble (two helpings).

Day 18 (Clathy to Cleish - 19 miles)

My big breakfasts were becoming the norm but I would never turn down the opportunity, as my lunches were often sparse. Marv and I had both lost weight in the first two weeks and it was my chance to put some back on. We crossed the busy A9 just north of Auchterarder, and actually rode through Dunning where we had had drinks the night before. Dunning is a lovely picturesque village and I stopped at the Post Office for some lunch supplies and some mints for Marv. Some of the locals came to say hello and proceeded to buy Marv a big bag of apples which I fed to him for the next few hours. We then took the steep single track road southeast out of Dunning, which climbed to 251 metres. There were good views northeast to Perth, but the road was like a roller coaster and I was more focused on the route ahead than looking back. We dropped down into the hamlet of Pathstruie which felt like the back of beyond. Climbing again out of the hamlet up to 273 metres and having 'fun' with the local bin lorry which kept overtaking us. Marv didn't seem to mind today and ignored it thankfully. We then passed a herd of Highland cows getting their hooves trimmed by a farrier or vet in a field. The rest of the route today was very zigzag until we came out of the wooded Ochil Hills and the roads become flatter for the last two hours.

Due to the number of hills we had climbed today the 19 miles took a fair time and we were very glad to reach my cousin Rory's house in Cleish. They luckily had some stables and a field. Marv was duly fed first and Rory had kindly organised a family get together that night. Joining Rory and his wife Laurie were; Rory's brother Jamie and his wife Sarah, Fi and Maisie and family friends Dennis and Jean. I had a fair bit to drink over dinner, and afterwards we went out to see Marv to introduce him to everyone. I decided to demonstrate how safe Marv was by cantering him bareback round the field with no reins or head collar. He did a great job for the audience, but he did look a bit bemused as to why I was doing this in his down time! It was great to catch up with them all and let my hair down a little.

With Rory and Laurie (and mooch)

Day 19 (Cleish to Dunfermline - 16 miles)

Marv has become an expert at grazing on the hoof. He is a verge expert and always keeps an eye out for a spot of clover which he can dive into and devour. I am keen that he does snack during the day to keep up his energy and actively encourage this. I would often take a break and sit down on the verge whilst he hoovered up as much grass as he could in the ten minutes he had. Sometimes he went for higher vegetation and grabbed at branches. He didn't stop walking but just lunged to the side and ripped the branches off on the move. I called these his leaf kebabs. Sometimes when I turned around there was an end of a branch poking out each side of his mouth as he chewed his way along it. I then helped him out by pulling one end and he stripped the rest of the leaves off.

We left Cleish armed with a huge packed lunch thanks to Rory. The route led due south again climbing to 282 metres through a big forestry block. We were shadowing the M90 which ran a few miles to the east. The last few miles today took us through Townhill on the outskirts of Dunfermline. Mum and Ken lived in Dunfermline and that is where I was staying later. We had to skirt round the edges of town as I didn't fancy taking on the busy town traffic. I found a disused railway line which helped, but I struggled a little in suburbia and found navigation much easier in the countryside. We found Ian and Pat's farm at Masterton which overlooked the Forth bridges. These were friends of Mum and Ken and they had kindly allowed Marv to stay in a stable. Once Marv was fed and watered I was driven back by Mum and Ken to their house for a bath and supper. Rob, who I had seen a few days earlier joined us for dinner along with Mark (the website wizard), Fi and Maisie. I now had had two great social evenings back to back and I was feeling really positive. I had managed to get Marv and myself back to Edinburgh from the top of Scotland, on schedule and in a fit state. I still had to get over the Forth Road Bridge, which I thought might be tricky.

Dinner with Mum, Ken, Rob and Mark at Dunfermline

Day 20 (Dunfermline to Balerno/Edinburgh - 16 miles)

I was dropped off at Masterton by the team and I saddled up Marv for the bridge attempt. We had a back-up plan of Rob driving a borrowed 4x4 with a borrowed horse trailer if the crossing was unsuccessful. Ken had recce'd the best approach route to the bridge which was through the Bridge Hotel car park. A path led from the car park straight on to the footpath of the bridge. Before I knew it we were on the bridge and I was leading Marv in quite windy conditions. My heart was racing as I knew there might be an issue. There was no sign to say no horses, and the Forth crossing website also had no rules for horses, so I felt I had just cause. Also just to add pressure, Ken had called STV and tipped them off and so they were waiting on the far side of the bridge to interview me. Marv was on his toes and was looking around at the great view, but he was not panicking and we made good progress.

We reached the half-way point and a car came towards us on the footpath with its lights flashing. Here we go, Bridge authority vehicle approaching. The car stopped alongside and the driver said something inaudible through the lowered window, which I didn't catch due to the gusty wind. I shrugged and said that there was no sign to say no horses and carried on. He drove off northbound. As we approached the south side of the bridge I could see a police car waiting for me with the blue lights flashing. Oh dear! Also there was an STV cameraman set up filming me approaching. I put on a brave face and strode on towards them both. A reporter came forward and interviewed me as I left the bridge. After which a policeman approached and stopped me. It appears that the Bridge authority was not happy, as apparently there was an unadvertised bye law that forbade livestock, which apparently I should have known about (not sure how?). I told him I was doing the trip for charity and that I was to be on this evening's news. He understood and told me to carry on while he sorted out the nonsense with the over officious Bridge authority.

(L) On the Forth Road Bridge, (R) South Queensferry and the Forth (rail) Bridge

Later in the year, the Bridge authority actually put up barriers at each end, possibly to prevent a re-occurrence of our crossing (it may have just been a coincidence). I still don't think they have put up a no-horses sign. It could be that Marv was the last ever horse to cross the Forth Road Bridge on foot...? Once over the bridge I still had to do a photo call at the Mace office (near the Airport). Mace wanted to do a news story on their employee and so I turned up in the car park and all the staff came out for a mass photo with Marv. STV were also there to complete the interview. I stupidly forgot to take my Oakley sunglasses off and put my helmet on, so looked a proper cowboy on TV which was not very clever. I had taken a lightweight climbing helmet with me, and the helmet travelled the whole trip with me, but was not used a great deal. After leaving Mace I headed through Heriot Watt University's campus and finally reached the organised field between Balerno and Currie on the outskirts of Edinburgh. Charlene was the field owner and had a three year old long legged Clydesdale neighbour for Marv called Goofy. It was then back to our house in Morningside (where the trip was planned) for two blissful days off.

Day 21 (Balerno/Edinburgh - rest day)

We got up early to go out and see Marv. I had been waking at 0500 on average and would often start a day at 0600 if I was not someone's guest. So a lie in to 0700 was allowed. We were met at the field by some local children who had seen Marv on the news and were keen to know more about him and the trip. Similarly, Fi and Mark had been receiving well-wishers messages from all over, some even from overseas. They would then add the kind words to the respective website page which gave me more encouragement that the trip was indeed a worthwhile venture.

Marv enjoys a good roll near Balerno

Day 22 (Balerno/Edinburgh - rest day)

Another relaxing day was had, continuing to plan and book more fields/stables for Marv for the forthcoming weeks' travels. I had a large section of northern and central England with no fields booked (most of my organised horse accommodation was in central Scotland, Shropshire, Gloucestershire and Wiltshire). I also had nothing organised for the last two weeks in the southwest of England. This I did deliberately to ensure some uncertainty remained and thus maintaining the sense of adventure.

Week 4 (106 miles)

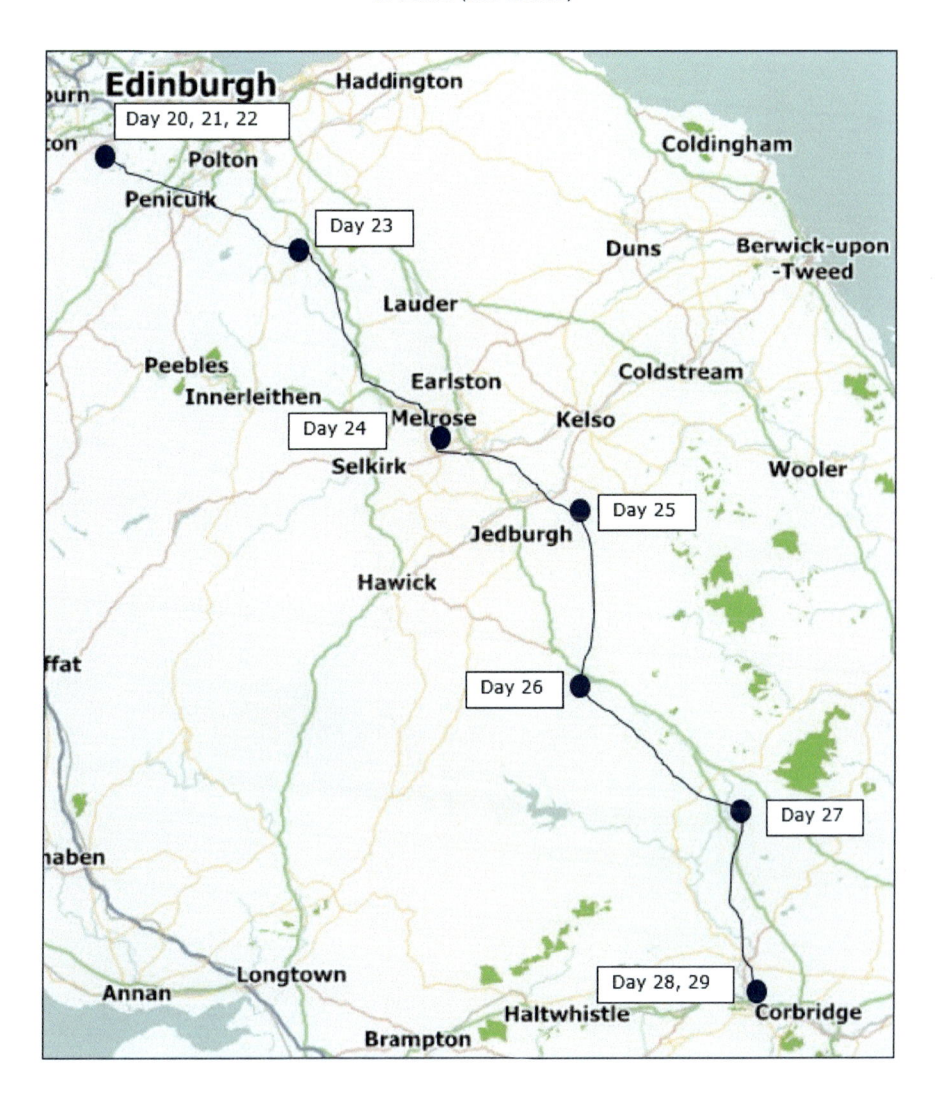

Week 4 (total 106 miles)

Day 23 (Edinburgh to Heriot - 19 miles)

When Fi and I came up to the field on the Monday morning, Marv was lying flat out and looking very relaxed. He popped up his head long enough to register us then flopped back into repose. I think he thought the trip was over after having a long restful weekend and back in his own territory. We sent Maisie over to say hello, and with a grunt Marv got up and wandered over. Today's ride would take us over the Pentland Hills and into the Scottish Borders. I knew the first part of the ride well, as we had walked and cycled the route a few times before.

Maisie joined us for the full day and we set off up the climb and managed a photo on the highest part of the pass looking back at Edinburgh and the Firth of Forth. We dropped down the far side into Glencorse, passed next to the reservoir and Flotterstone Inn. It was then a quick spell on the verge of the busy A702 before heading onto the back roads again around Glencorse Barracks. The route took us very close to Gorebridge and some of the miles were over roads Marv and I had trained on during our build up weekends. I think Marv found the area familiar.

(L) & (R) Heading over the Pentland Hills

It was at this point that John, my manager at Mace, who had authorised my leave of absence to undertake the trip, and his wife met up with us. He had packed an awesome picnic into the boot of his car with numerous snacks for Marv too. We found a suitable layby with a grassy verge to catch up and talk about the trip. After lunch, as we passed through Middleton, we were on new ground again and the last few miles of the day used an old Roman Road route across the fields to Heriot. The views were spectacular and we cantered through fields with cows and sheep around us. Marv was a bit wary of the cows as they started to follow us, but Maisie thought the whole episode was great fun. My friend Julian (our website diary editor) had parked at Heriot and walked out to meet up with us coming in. Janet from Heriot had kindly allowed us a field for Marv and a nice spot to pitch the tents. Julian was joining us for the night and was camping too. Fi arrived after work and we pitched the two tents. Maisie was really tired as she was not used to a full day's travels and she went straight to sleep for a rest. Janet generously brought out some brandy and ginger ale and we went up the field to say hello to her horses and Marv. Marv was in a separate field to her horses, and he was already becoming friendly with the mare. Later on the three of us headed to a local pub in Middleton for a meal before going to do a final check on Marv. Marv who had already jumped out of his field, was now in with the two other horses! Janet moved her gelding (William) out to prevent a fight and Marv got to spend the night with his new female friend. We let Julian have Maisie in his tent for the night.

(Clockwise from top left) Arriving at Heriot, Marv checks out his competition, Marv necking his special mare and Marv in contemplation

Day 24 (Heriot to Melrose - 19 miles)

Marv and Maisie share breakfast

Janet appeared early the next day with a tray of bacon, toast and coffee. A superb start to the morning. We packed up the tents and went to grab Marv, who would not be caught today. Normally he would come straight over to be saddled up, but today he needed some persuasion to even get a head collar on. Once we started leading him out of the field he then pulled away and escaped back to the mare. Finally we got him down to the road and equipment fitted. I said my farewells and headed south, this time without the Mooch. The route was very scenic and shadowed the Gala Water and A7. Marv continually stopped, looked round and neighed loudly for the first mile. He had certainly fallen for the mare from Heriot. Once we had put some miles in he settled down and we managed some lengthy trots as we neared Galashiels. After passing the Gala rugby ground we headed along the disused railway line which connects Galashiels to Melrose. Again, we made good time by cantering on the level surface and passing a few dog walkers and cyclists at speed.

A friend of mine, Jamie, had asked his wife Mhairi to meet us in Melrose town centre and she showed me to a field they had secured on the eastern edge of town. The field had some horses in it already and I was concerned that a kick from either of them could end the trip, as they did not take very kindly to Marv. However, the landowner was not there to discuss this issue and so I felt obliged to put him where I was told. It was then back to Jamie's house, where I managed a shower and a mini siesta before Fi and Maisie arrived. They were to join us for dinner. We headed out to see Marv after the meal and decided that the horses were still not getting on well, so I moved Marv to another field nearby just in case.

Day 25 (Melrose to Oxnam - 19 miles)

This was to be our last full day in Scotland. After breakfast, Fi and Maisie headed north back to Edinburgh and I bade farewell to Jamie, Mhairi and their young son Innes and set off south east towards Jedburgh. I put some sun tan lotion on Marv's pink patches on his nose, which he disliked intensely, but if not applied would have resulted in sunburn and a scabby face. We stopped in the quaint village of St Boswells for a snack restock and pit stop for Marv's mints, carrots and an apple. Shortly afterwards I made an error in directional choice by deciding to use a public footpath as an alternative route. The path was too narrow for a horse and saddlebags, and ended with a footbridge which was useless. We managed a tight U turn but on the way back one of the saddle bags ripped open as we squeezed through. All the contents spilled out onto the path. I was annoyed at myself for taking the wrong route and then for the ensuing kit disaster. I managed to stuff the spilled kit into the day sack that I had, and we carried on the pre-planned horse friendly route. Mental note; footpaths are footpaths for a reason, otherwise they would be bridleways. This was a good lesson to learn!

The day improved and we made some good speed with numerous trots and canters past the dominant Waterloo war memorial monument on the hill. We had our lunch break today deep in a grassy bottomed forest. I just lay down for 30 minutes shuteye, whilst Marv munched his way around me. We had to take a slight detour to cross the River Teviot as the bridge I had picked was not suitable for horses. The final leg of the day picked up the old Roman Road again (called 'Dere Street') which was straight but quite rocky. Dere Street took me right to Polly's steading, who had kindly allowed Marv a stable and me a bed. Before dinner, Polly took me to a local equestrian store where their resident saddler repaired my ripped saddle bag. I met the kids back at the steading and managed to build a Lego tank for Angus which he promised to take to school the next day to show his school friends. I then spent a very relaxed night with the family eating a lovely venison casserole and rhubarb crumble. Polly gave me some tips for the next day's route out of Scotland.

Great moustache

Day 26 (Oxnam to Cottonshopeburnfoot - 14 miles)

Although the mileage was comparatively low today, we were going to be doing most of the miles off road. We bade farewell to Polly and family before re-joining Dere Street. This leg was in my top five most memorable sections of the trip. I was on a Roman road heading towards the border with England, just as many others will have done in centuries past. Dere Street was grassed over and the ride was spectacularly scenic. A few remote farms and barns were the only signs of habitation. A dry stone wall ran alongside part of the way, and I came across a solitary man working on rebuilding a section of the wall.

Heading into the Cheviots whilst using the spectacular Roman Road

We were now deep in the Cheviot Hills climbing up towards the border at approximately 400 metres. The other side of the border was Otterburn Military Training Area where I had spent some time on exercise in the Army a decade ago. We reached the inconspicuous Scotland / England border, which was marked only by a fence line and a small signpost. It also was located in a peat bog, so crossing here was especially difficult. We spent quite some time trying to find a suitably firm route through. I did not want a repeat of day four and getting Marv stuck on the border miles from any help. On reflection, I would not repeat this route over the border with a horse, as the ground was too soft, but luck was on our side and we just made it through.

(L) Last view of Scotland, (R) crossing into England adjacent to Otterburn Training area

The red military range flags were flying off to our left and we skirted round the area closely following the edge of a forestry block beginning our descent down to the A68. On the way down through a steep section of forestry we met, coming up the way, an inspiration in the form of Scott Cunningham and his dog Travis and a couple of military assistants. They were walking the length of the Pennine Way (this was part of the last section), and Scott was blind. They were raising money for Guide Dogs for the Blind. I was left humbled as we parted. Once we managed to complete the descent, we found the A68 and a road side service station with a cafe provided more sustenance. From there it was a short hop to the Border Forest caravan park at Cottonshopeburnfoot (great name). The owners had agreed to let Marv have a field for the night. Fi and Maisie had managed another Friday off and came down to join me for the long weekend. We pitched the tent in the same (stream side) field so we could keep an eye on Marv and the two shy Alpacas in the adjacent field.

Day 27 (Cottonshopeburnfoot to Woodburn, nr Bellingham - 15 miles)

Sun cream application

In the morning, Marv was being bothered by midges and so we quickly packed up the tent and I headed off with Marv and Maisie. To get out of the caravan site, we had to exit a tight gate, which necessitated taking off all the saddle bags to get through (only one minute after departure). That was a bit embarrassing with all the resident campers watching. We re-joined the Pennine way heading south, which was a stony forest track, the first type of ground that Marv did not like. We had to go quite slowly and keep to the verges as the stones were getting stuck in his shoes. Finally the stones stopped and the tracks became grassy which allowed for some fast canters. Maisie had to run flat out to keep up and I got a great photo of her sprinting just by my side with all four paws outstretched in a superman pose.

(L) Maisie at speed at the canter, (R) road junction near Bellingham

Fi arranged to meet me at a remote junction of the B6320 at Hareshaw Head (311m). From here it was 3.5 miles to Yellow House Farm. Fi had parked at the farm and the owner Avril then offered Fi a lift out to meet me so we could share a few miles together. It was great to have her alongside us as she put so much into the trip and it wouldn't have happened without her. I ensured she got a well-deserved ride on Marv over Corsenside Common.

Final miles of the day into Woodburn

Yellow House Farm was a horse friendly B&B, and Marv had the biggest field of the trip, at least 20 acres of lush grass. For the first time, he ignored his evening meal and just cantered off up the field into the distance. I took it personally that he had ignored me and shot off, and I then had a subdued evening as a consequence. As we had made good time today we headed off to the local town of Hexham for some essential shopping and repairs. My saddlebags needed adjusting to Marv's changing body shape, and so Derek's shoe bar offered to fix this for me. I bought a map I needed and some replacement trousers due to the first pair being beyond repair now. We had dinner in the local pub 'The Bay Horse' (aptly named) and it was Fi and Maisie who went to check on Marv.

Day 28 (Woodburn to Anick, nr Hexham - 20 miles)

As expected in a B&B we had a comprehensive cooked breakfast and cereal to start the day. We learnt that Avril's father had been Master of the local Haydon hunt for 20 years and in the guesthouse there were some wonderful pictures and paintings depicting him hunting. Fi went over to get Marv from the far end of the field, which took her 15 minutes to do. Marv and I made up and I gave him a big hug. We were back friends again. I am not sure why he was in a huff with me the night before. I guess we all get bad days. We set off for Anick Grange B&B, which was just north of Hexham near the A69. The route bypassed Bellingham and took the winding back roads next to the River North Tyne. We also found a disused railway line to use which was perfect for some cantering.

We had agreed to meet at a village called Birtley for lunch. Fi had a good picnic in the boot of the car and we let Marv loose in the walled village green while we had our sandwiches. We didn't take Marv's saddle off, but just loosened the girth at little. After Marv had eaten his hard feed he moved off to munch grass. Then as we watched, his legs started to buckle. Both Fi and I jumped up and shouted at Marv as he was preparing to have a roll in the grass. Marv got quite a shock and stood up straight and looked very startled. Had he gone down, this would have likely broken the saddle and jeopardised the trip. Off came the saddle, and Marv duly had his roll.

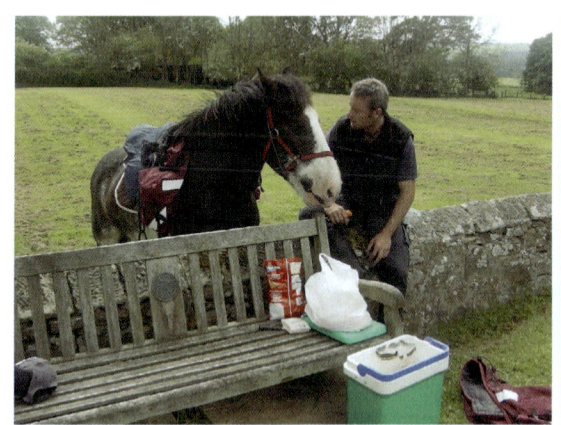

(L) Picnic lunch at Birtley, (R) heading off afterwards

Shortly after lunch I was tracked down by a University friend's parents who had a house near Kielder Water. Nick's folks knew my route and timings and just drove round the corner and found us on the move. It was good to catch up with them as I had stayed with Nick a few times during our University days. We passed Chipchase and Haughton Castles and then crossed the line of Hadrian's Wall at

Walwick (which was the location for a Roman Fort and Mile Castle no. 28), just after crossing the Tyne. All very fortified round here!

I had then agreed to meet Fi at Keepwick Fell four miles north of the B&B. Fi duly made the rendezvous and found me, Marv and Maisie motoring on. I needed to utilise what I termed the 'speedy stick' as Marv was taking the P with his pace a little. A speedy stick is any stick, which if waved or seen by Marv, induces an increase in speed without any contact needing to be made. Later in the trip proximity to pigs would have the same effect.

(L) Marv waited outside this Post Office whilst I got snacks, (R) munching verge whilst Maisie keep a close eye

It was quite a long day and I was glad of the company for the last few miles. Maisie had done well in joining me for the second half of the day. We met Julie, the owner of the equine B&B, and were given an excellent field for Marv, accessed through the garden. After sorting out Marv and putting away the kit, we showered and headed to the local inn 'The Rat' for some scoff. We were to spend two nights in Anick as we had earned a day off on the Sunday. Staying at the B&B felt like pure luxury and maybe not fully in the original spirit of the trip, but after Monday night Fi was heading north and I would not see her again until Worcester. She had supported me and seen me through the first four weeks superbly, and had driven hundreds of miles to share the first four weekends with Marv and me, sorting out numerous nights' welcome accommodation.

Day 29 (Hexham - rest day)

We had a long lie in and a relaxing breakfast before heading back in to Hexham for another look around. I spent some time getting my diary up to speed, so that Fi could take my scribbles back to Edinburgh and convert it to legible text to be uploaded to the website. Writing the diary was something I did do every day despite how tired I was, as I did not want to miss detailing any part of the trip. This is probably partly why, seven years on, I have decided to complete this process of recording in the format of a book. I tidied up the maps from week four and bundled them up for Fi to take home, while I looked over the next bundle of maps. My plan was to carry a week's worth of maps at a time. They were quite heavy, and so for later weeks, I had sent some bundles of maps to pre-planned addresses to be collected on route.

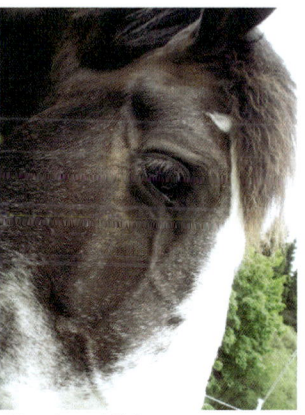

Marv enjoys his field at Anick, Maisie enjoys Marv's saddlebags

Week 5 (104 miles)

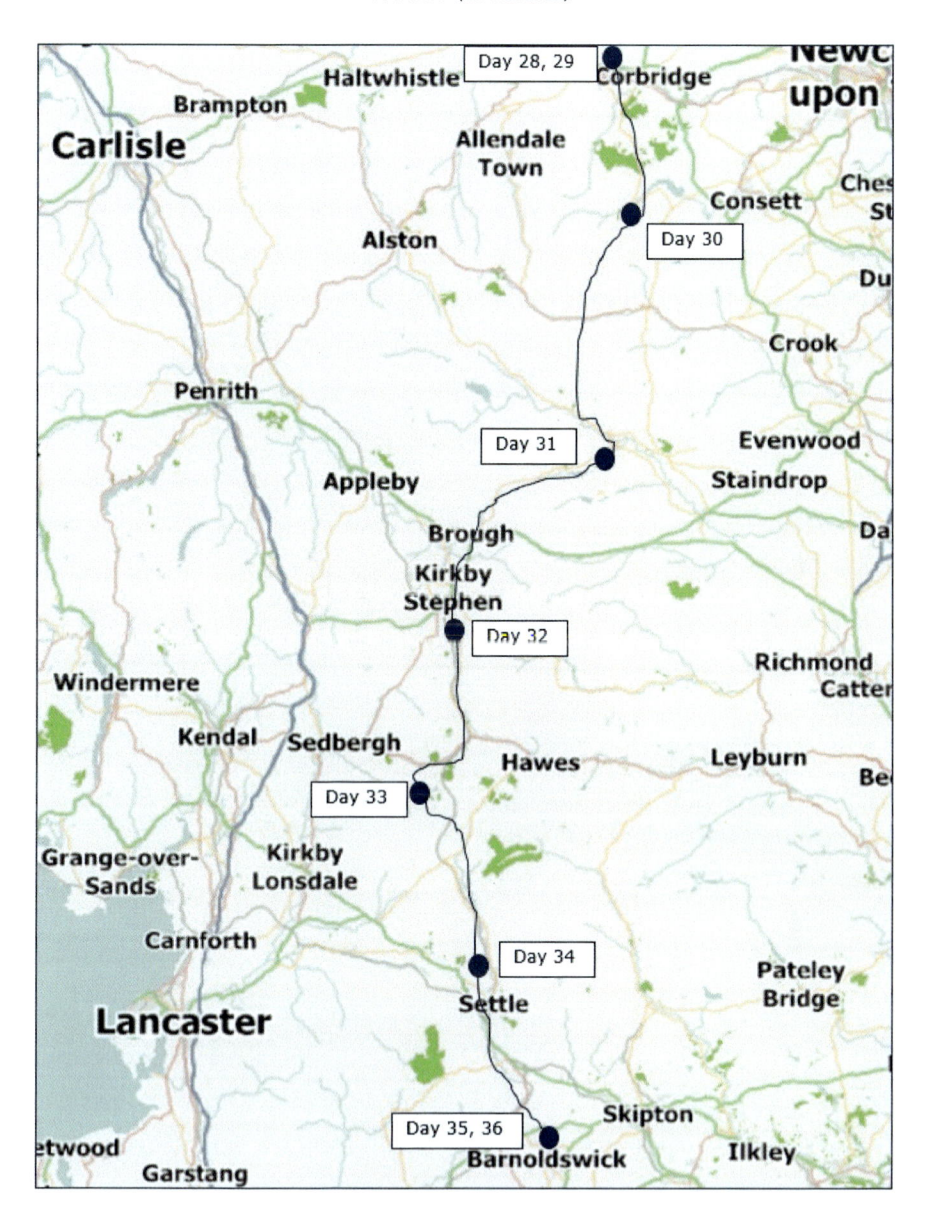

Week 5 (total 104 miles)

<u>Day 30 (Hexham to Rookhope - 19 miles)</u>

Marv was on fine form today, whinnying for his breakfast of Staypower muesli. He was waiting at the gate raring to go and this meant a lot to me, that Marv was very likely enjoying the trip too and was keen for the next leg. After breakfast, I trotted Marv into Hexham town centre, through the streets and back out into the countryside, after which I was joined by Maisie as the roads became quieter. We were heading for a village called Blanchland (which was my intended night stop). Today was only planned to be 14 miles and the next day was a planned 24 miler. When I pondered this again, this seemed very unbalanced. So midway through the morning I called Fi to tell her I would be pushing on to Rookhope to even out the distances over the two days. She had already been to Blanchland and secured a field for Marv, so I apologised and asked her if she could possibly try Rookland. Maisie managed to get stung in the eye again and I met up with Fi on the corner of a forestry block to hand over the dog and have some lunch. Marv started to attempt to sneak back the way he came instead of just his usual grazing so we cut the lunch short and pressed on.

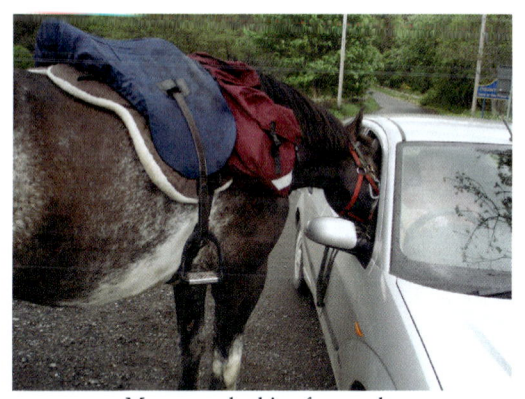

Marv goes looking for snacks

We met up again later at Townfield, and Maisie's eye was vastly improved. Marv spotted Fi in the car and trotted over and stuck his massive head into the driver's window to look for food. Maisie's morale was back and so she joined me for the last five miles over Hunstanworth Moor (500m). We had now left Northumberland and were in County Durham, and it was good to be making real progress south. The area was spectacularly beautiful, but this came at a price of being very hilly with plenty of steady climbs to contend with adding to the travelling time. Fi came to meet me at the summit of the moor to tell me that she had found a friendly farmer Ian, in Rookhope, who kindly let us have a field to camp in and graze Marv overnight, and that was very welcome news. We shared the field with Marv and an assortment of sheep and chickens which certainly amused Maisie, who had to be cautioned not to herd the sheep and worry the poultry. She was then seen off by a particularly fierce ewe putting an end to her shenanigans, as she ran around behind Marv for protection. We had the use of an outbuilding to store the saddle and gear, and this also came with an outside loo and running hot water (bonus!). As the weather was not favourable it was great to be able to cook our evening meal inside the outbuilding, as the tent was a bit cramped for the stove. Later on we met Ian's wife Jackie and her daughters, who had just returned from a county show. They were pleased to see Marv and hear all about his tales.

Is there room in the tent for us?

Day 31 (Rookhope to Middleton in Teesdale - 20 miles)

Fi had to leave very early to get back to her job in Edinburgh. Marv and I bade a sad farewell to Fi and the Mooch, who had kept up our spirits continually. With the tent gone too, I had a few extra hours kipping in the outhouse. The rain and wind had increased and so I moved Marv into an empty stable for an hour before we started off. I started to feel the apprehension again as I was heading into the unknown territory of the north of England, with only a couple of fields organised. My next 'well booked' section was Shropshire and Worcestershire still a few weeks away.

I pulled on the waterproofs. Marv and I headed south somewhat down spirited, and to top it all I was feeling ill for the first time on the trip. I was so glad I had done some extra miles yesterday as I found today one of the toughest. Our route took us through, up and over Lintzgarth Common and into Westgate (which is high up in the Wear valley). The roads were too steep to trot and so the miles came slowly. After Westgate it was up over Swinhope Moor (609m). My memory of this day is limited as I mentally shut down and just plodded on in the rain, just concentrating on navigating to the next checkpoint and paying little regard to my surroundings. We dropped down into Newbiggin, where I had a sleep by the side of the road whilst Marv munched verge. I was dehydrated and needed to pull myself together a bit. We pushed on and made the lovely village of Middleton in Teesdale. I wish I could have appreciated it a bit more, as we strode through and out again for another four miles on the B6276, to find Les Spark who is the man behind Free N' Easy saddles.

With Les at his home near Middleton in Teesdale

Les had warmly offered Marv a field and me a bed en route. I was very relieved to reach his farmhouse and steading which served as his workshop. Marv was turned out into an adjacent dry stone walled paddock. After a shower and some much needed sustenance, Les showed me his workshop, where my saddle was made, and we talked for ages on how Marv and I had got on to date. I raved about the saddle, knowing that Marv's back was in great condition with no soreness or rubs.

Les was counting on this too, as he had used our trip to help advertise the benefits of his type of saddle construction. I am surprised that not more saddles are made in this style, as the military have used similar saddles successfully for centuries. Yet in the last 50 years that knowledge seems to have been forgotten by most. What Les has done has improved upon a tried and tested saddle construction method, allowing easy adjustment of the saddle by the rider. This enables the saddle to change with the horse as the horse's back muscles evolve, and also means that the saddle can fit a variety of horses easily. Les is also a successful long distance rider himself, and he has proved that his own saddles are successful by undertaking hundreds of miles of testing. Les took the saddle and looked at it on Marv, then brought it into the workshop to ensure it was adjusted correctly. It seemed I hadn't done a bad job of self-adjustment on route. Whilst there, I also purchased a neoprene girth for Marv, as I thought he would benefit from it.

Day 32 (Middleton in Teesdale to Kirby Stephen - 16 miles)

During the previous evening over a few glasses of wine, I had noted to Les that Marv's front shoes would need replacing soon. They had lasted almost 500 miles and is a testament to Donald, our Edinburgh farrier, who used to be in the Army and still shoed the Police horses. He had used special tungsten tipped road nails to minimise the wear on them. Les found out that his local farrier William was to be shoeing nearby today and could squeeze Marv in for a set. We had to box Marv over to the farm as it was a few miles away. Marv wasn't keen to be loaded up and needed a little encouragement to get up the ramp. Logically, in these parts, the farriers ask that if local horses need shoeing that they congregate at set locations so they didn't have to drive around and lose valuable time. We were put to the front of the queue and it was great to meet other horse owners who had travelled over to get their horses re-shod and talk through our travels. Once he had his new pair of shoes, he reloaded ok, and we drove back to Low Selset.

We didn't set off until midday, and I was still not 100% ok, but certainly better from having had a hot shower and a bed. We headed west on the B road passing Selset reservoir steadily climbing to 482 metres, with Warcop (ranges) danger area ahead of us. This is where I completed the P Company 20 miler back in 1998 and I thought it fitting I was back in the area doing another 20 miler, but with a horse and saddlebags instead of a rifle and a bergen. The moorland road was very remote and we didn't see much until we reached Brough (pronounced bruff I believe). I found a shop and bought us some lunch and horse snacks. The food and rest helped re-energise us, before we tackled the last few miles to Kirby. Just after setting off, I bumped into an Artillery officer in his Army landrover (Capt Wall from 12 Regt) and our chat gave me another boost. I had hoped to take a circuitous scenic route via Great Musgrave, but the extra mile that that would have entailed swung it for me, and I opted for the direct A685 road instead. Looking back now, that was a bit poor, but I just wasn't in the right mood for sightseeing. So we used the wide grassy verge and we did a great deal of cantering alongside the traffic to speed our way to the town.

Kirby Stephen is a smart little town in Cumbria and it had a very relaxed feel to it. After a quick stop in its local supermarket for supplies, we then headed south out of town looking for a suitable field for Marv. We took the Nateby road and I stopped at the first farm opposite the local pub. We were now very close to Appleby, which was due to hold its famous horse fair in a week's time. I was aware of the large quantity of travelling folk heading north to rendezvous for this equine gathering, and people were beginning to warn me of the likelihood of meeting some of them. They do get a bad name and I was just concerned that Marv might go missing during the night only to be found pulling a caravan in the opposite direction!

I met Malcolm the local farmer who offered Marv a field. After supper in the pub I retired back to my bivi and Malcolm came over to sit with me for a while. We had a poignant chat watching Marv grazing and mixing with his sheep. Later on I kept checking throughout the night from my sleeping bag that Marv was still grazing nearby.

(L) Marv explores the barn, (R) Marv comes looking for his evening treats under the bivi

Day 33 (Kirby Stephen to Cowgill - 16 miles)

I woke early to find Marv still eating close by. Relaxing somewhat, I had a lie in as Marv continued to stock up on the green calories. I had a tasty breakfast of Alpen and powdered milk, before collapsing the bivi and packing away the gear into the saddle bags. As soon as my packing was completed, Marv casually strolled over and just stood for me while I saddled him up. This was fantastic as it meant he knew his job and we didn't have to communicate to know what was required.

As we left Nateby we followed the River Eden, and the road ran alongside the line of the Settle to Carlisle steam railway for a good distance. We were passed by the steam train puffing its way north, whereby Marv's eyes nearly popped out as he froze and prepared to make a dash for it. I utilised his sudden spurt of energy and we trotted fast for a mile or until he was sure he was safe. It was along this scenic section that we also were treated to a free air display of RAF Tornadoes, a Spitfire and Apache helicopters. A real bonus for me, but Marv was unconcerned.

Marv tries trainspotting

The rain started in earnest and we stopped periodically under trees and in abandoned barns for the heavy showers to pass. Marv was also freaked out when we met a gypsy caravan coming towards us heading for Appelby. I stopped to chat and they were friendly enough. I didn't say too much about where I was headed, just in case. Finally we reached the solitary Moorcock Inn at the junction of the A684, and I left Marv outside whilst I managed to nip in and grab a takeaway baguette. After which, we did one mile on the A road before turning left at Garsdale Head station and heading up a monstrously steep (two chevron) incline over Garsdale Common.

150 metres of ascent over just 1km was testing, but was eased by meeting up with my godparents Chris and Graham. Graham dropped off Christine to walk the last few miles with me to their house in Cowgill. As usual, Marv was given snacks a plenty and as we descended into Dentdale the view was stunning. The railway line ran through a long tunnel under the hill (the one we had climbed) to reappear at

Dent station (the highest in the UK at 350 metres) which we passed by on the steep descent down the Coal Road. Two miles on, we arrived at East Stone House, where I had stayed many times as a child, en route on our many trips to Scotland for holidays. It was unusual arriving by horse and from a different direction. Chris and Graham didn't have a field but Marv was allowed free access to their garden (a brave choice), and he happily roamed around the house nibbling grass and looking in at us inside. I grabbed a bath and a siesta before being able to be more sociable and catch up with my hosts properly. I turned in early after dinner with a headache and sore feet and a need to make the most of the bed.

(L) On the bridge by Dent station with Chris, (R) Marv in East Stone House garden

Day 34 (Cowgill to Stainforth, Nr Settle - 16 miles)

After breakfast we set off and were joined by both Chris and Graham for an hour and a neighbour's West Highland terrier Missie. We passed alongside a fabulous limestone bedded crystal clear stream, where the rocks had been eroded away leaving amazing natural shapes. I said farewell to Chris after passing under the viaduct and Graham walked me to the top of Newby Head (411m), before I turned south for Ribblesdale. This road was just as scenic as anything so far, with the Settle – Carlisle railway line joining us again across the Dales. It was certainly dry stone wall territory, with walls to be seen enclosing sheep in every direction.

The road was popular with touring motorbikes, but Marv had by now realised that they were nothing to be afraid of and just ignored them as they passed by. The day was sunny and bright with loads of people picnicking in the vicinity of Ribblehead viaduct. I took the opportunity to call James, a good friend from University with whom I had also spent five months backpacking, to congratulate him on his recent Mt Everest ascent. We had almost met up when I passed nearby a few days earlier, but he wasn't back in the country until I was out of Cumbria.

Ribbleshead viaduct

We passed the nearby remote railway station which was buzzing with tourists and continued to follow the railway line south passing Ingleborough hill (724m) which lay to the west of us. We pit stopped in Horton in Ribblesdale, which was quaint and certainly geared up for the summer tourist traffic. The B6479 we were on was getting busier with an increasing number of speeding lorries servicing a local quarry. I was now quite concerned about our safety, as these lorries were flying along going over blind summits and we could not get out of the way very quickly. We trotted on as fast as we could all the while keeping an ear out for the next suicidal HGV to potentially run us over. Finally and with great relief, we got off the road into the village of Stainforth, the scheduled village for tonight. I asked around and a kind Mr Hennigham allowed the use of a field for us both. The field had very long grass, and at times I couldn't even see Marv as he worked his way around the field sampling Yorkshire's finest greenery. It was no fancy food for me tonight, just the tried and tested noodles in a mess tin. Marv was heard later that night snoring deeply, so he must have found the deep grass to his complete satisfaction.

Day 35 (Stainforth to Barnoldswick - 17 miles)

The last day of week five and a final push to Barnoldswick. Marv woke me early with his nose coming into my bivi looking for his breakfast. All I had was wine gums, which he took anyway, but I think he was missing the muesli mix which he had enjoyed for many days in the early weeks. I managed to get off the nasty A road and find a scenic single track west of the River Ribble (it was called the Ribble Way). This sleepy road was ideal and we passed through the edge of the town of Settle early on Saturday morning. There was no one around and the place felt uninhabited, but we just pushed on south staying on the quiet side of the valley. We passed through Wigglesworth where we spotted a horse spa and it was tempting to check Marv in for a treatment. It was soon after that, being a hot day, I stopped at a pub and asked for a bucket of water for Marv. He simply turned his nose up at it. You can lead a horse to water.........

Then Mark and his girlfriend Vicky arrived from Edinburgh. Mark's family is from Lancashire (not too far from here apparently) and he was down seeing them and would be spending the night with Marv and I. We had lunch in a nice picnic area with Marv roaming free in the enclosure. Vicky had brought Marv strawberries, one of his favourites, and this left him with a very red mouth and 'heavy horse' moustache. As we left the field I dropped my gilet but neglected to pick it up as I led Marv out onto the road. He predictably walked over it, and then I remembered that I had my camera in the pocket. El stupido. It was broken, and Vicky very kindly offered to drive to the nearest Argos in Skipton to replace it. I cussed myself but carried on heading south whilst Mark and Vicky shot off to look for a possible field for the night.

When I was going through the non-descript Barnoldswick they both found me again and Mark was dropped off to join me heading towards Salterforth. They had organised a field there for Marv at a large livery yard run by Jackie and Howard. As we walked into the yard all the stable girls came out to greet us and they rushed over to say hello to Marv. The yard let us use the powerful hose to give Marv his first proper shampoo and clean. Then he was turned out into a large field. He had plenty of other horses in adjoining fields for company as well as us camping in the same field. Mark had also brought down my tent so I could have a night in relative comfort. We pitched the tents in a corner of Marv's field next to some show jumps, and Mark cooked us a hearty supper using his camping gas cooker. We then headed off to the local Anchor for a drink and blether.

Day 36 (Barnoldswick - day off)

Marv was up first, trying my tent for his hard feed, but then spotting Mark, he walked over to his Land rover and spied the bag of feed in the back. Marv waited patiently until the bag was opened and he got his grub. After a well-earned lie in and campfire breakfast of bacon and eggs, Mark's parents popped in to wish us well. I really appreciated the effort so many people made to see us on the trip and share a part of it. We then headed off to Skipton for a tourists look around (including a barge trip) and a relaxing lunch. It was good to see a well-known town in Yorkshire without worrying where to tie up Marv.

A stop at a chip shop in Barnoldswick was in order before I was dropped off back in the field with Marv. Mark and Vicky left me so they could get back to Edinburgh, and I pitched my bivi using the show jumps for support. I couldn't use the fence this time as it was electrified. Mark and Vicky had kindly provided my next week's supply of maps, and I was able to hand over the last set of maps, together with diary notes and a memory stick of photos.

(L) Mark and Marv bonding, (R) my homemade bivi using show jump poles

Week 6 (120 miles)

- Day 35, 36 — Barnoldswick
- Day 37
- Day 38
- Day 39
- Day 40
- Day 41
- Day 42, 43

Week 6 (total 120 miles)

<u>Day 37 (Barnoldswick to Blackshaw head - 19 miles)</u>

I started Monday morning feeling a bit flat, as Mark and Vicky's company over the weekend had been uplifting, and it was now back to being on my own with Marv to push south through a part of Britain I hadn't experienced before. We were going to travel between the two large Victorian industrial towns of Burnley and Halifax. In effect, but not geographically, down the border between Lancashire and Yorkshire. It was a little daunting but also quite an exciting prospect.

Marv had woken me early by sticking his nose in the bivi and sniffing for his breakfast. I duly gave him his muesli to allow me another hour of rest. After getting up and concluding breakfast myself I was keen to get on the move. I quickly dismantled the lean to bivi and packed up the saddle bags. Marv was not keen on standing still this morning for the saddling up process. We were in a field with an electric fence running round it, so there were no obvious tying up points nearby. Being a bit too hasty, I thought that a large rubber bucket full of metal show jump cups would be a sufficient tying up point, as the bucket was quite heavy. Big mistake. Mid-way through the saddle fitting, Marv pulled back on the lead rope sufficiently for the bucket to jingle. The noise he took as a signal to rocket off round the field still attached to the bucket. On reflection I can now laugh, as Marv bucked and farted off with the bucket trailing between his legs, spilling metal cups as he went and then the saddle flew off (unbroken luckily). I could only watch feeling embarrassed with rising panic, imagining him getting into a real tangle. We were lucky, I caught Marv, calmed him down and extricated him from his bucket, tidied up the spilled cups and rapidly left. Luckily no one else saw the Benny Hill moment.

The weather was particularly hot today (being the start of June), and there was a fair bit of climbing to be done (up to 392m). Our route took us to the edge of the Pennines, which offered spectacular views. We stopped by Widdop reservoir mid-morning for Marv to get some grass, and I chatted to some young offenders who were out doing community service. They were quite interested in meeting Marv and hearing about his adventure. There were some great place names nearby as we passed through this area: Wicking Slack; The Notch; Clough Foot; Reap's Coppy and the aptly named Pack Horse Pub. At Gorple Lower reservoir I opted to follow the Pennine bridleway, which is a relatively new route. I have to say Marv did not enjoy some of the terrain, as it was very stony and sore on his feet. The road would have been quicker and flatter, but the views wouldn't have been the same. More climbing ensued and the bridleway improved to become grassy tracks, where I could urge Marv into some canters. The final climb to Blackshaw Head was quite hard, but worth the effort, as when we located the equine B&B, it offered superb views south over the next day's route. At the B&B Marv was initially offered a stable, but as he started using the partition as a scratching post and broke it, he was moved outside to a field. I spent the evening chatting to two couples who were walking the Pennine Way before getting to bed early.

Day 38 (Blackshaw Head to Diggle - 18 miles)

A very kind gentleman called Ralph had heard about the trip and had paid up front for me and Marv's stay at Badgers Field Farm. He was a fellow adventurer and turned up at breakfast on his classic Lee Enfield Bullet motorbike to meet me and share some stories. Ralph walked with me for the first half an hour's descent down to the Rochdale canal. Marv was quite quiet today and particularly responsive, probably mirroring my own mood. After climbing up the other side and following the Pennine bridleway, passing Todmorden down to our right, we descended back to the valley bottom. It was here I decided to change the route slightly and follow the canal towpath instead of climbing back up the other side on the Pennine bridleway. My logic was to stay on the flat and the average speed would then increase. I was soon to learn that the canal towpaths, designed a few hundred years ago for Marv's very type of horse, were now very much horse unfriendly. A very sad and demeaning state I would add. The canal path we managed to access was fantastic nonetheless. We were surrounded by classic Victorian industrial architecture, and it was easy to reminisce about the 19th century as we motored along. Marv and I managed many canters and fast trots past the old warehouses and wharfs.

We went under a few canal bridges, but one in particular stood out. The bridge had a very narrow, long dark tunnel next to the canal to go under a major road. Marv just fitted down the tunnel with his saddlebags, but it was a gamble to see how he reacted to this enclosed space. I led him down slowly, and he was calm as can be popping out the other side into daylight again. I was glad Marv still fully trusted in me despite our few mishaps to date. We reached a locked gate later on the canal, and after calling the number provided for British Waterways, I was told they would not open the gate for horses. Oh well, back onto the main road for a spell, to bypass this anti-horse section of canal path.

Great Pennine scenery

We did some urban navigating around Littleborough, (not enjoyable mixing with the traffic), and then headed back up the hill past Hollingworth Lake. This was an almost surreal mini water haven with people boating and eating ice creams only a mile from (and overlooking) an industrial town. We had to stop to take it all in and grab a snack. Shortly afterwards, we were back on the Pennine bridleway and passing under the busy M62 motorway, which towered above us on a huge viaduct. This was another seminal moment for me as it meant reaching the centre of the trip, roughly half way now, and putting behind me Scotland and the north of England. We were approaching the Midlands, with the southwest to follow.

The path was twisty and undulating with numerous climbs still to be tackled. We reached the A672 and near Denshaw I attempted to shortcut using a bridleway, which turned out to be impassable. This was to be a recurring theme and I soon tired of trying to use them, unless obviously usable. We then passed between the two Castleshaw reservoirs where I met up with Roger. We had first met Roger back at the campsite in Cottonshopeburnsfoot. He had offered for me to stay at his house in Diggle when we passed, and he had sorted out a field for Marv. Roger then joined us for the last few miles of the day. Roger's friend Lynn had kindly offered to look after Marv, and her friend Linda offered to wash the numnahs and other items. Fantastic. I left Marv at their yard and Roger drove me to his house nearby. Roger and Anna's house was beautiful and I was treated to a long hot bath, an amazing meal, and then a James Bond movie with Malt whisky to boot.

Day 39 (Diggle to Little Hayfield - 16 miles)

After a hugely comfortable night, and a 'monster' cooked breakfast, I felt fresh and raring to go. We drove back to the yard and thanked the ladies for their equine hospitality. Roger joined me for the first hour of the day, which followed the Pennine bridleway and former disused railway line, so it was fast, straight and level, the best you can get. Roger headed back at Greenfield, and we carried on the bridleway, making good time. The bridleway here is also named Tameside trail and Moor Edge road, which fairly described the route. We could see to our right the River Tame and Huddersfield Narrow canal, Mossley and Oldham and to our left the moors stretching out for miles. One of the best sections of our route I would say, as the scenery was picturesque, not too taxing in terms of gradient and the weather was fair. I then took another detour at Walkerwood Reservoir and headed south on minor roads through Matley and Mottram instead of going on the more circuitous Pennine bridleway loop which climbed to 311m. What I gained in time I certainly lost in views.

I met a guy called Dick when I stopped to buy some lunch in Mottram, and he kindly gave a donation and offered to find Marv a field for the night. I thanked him and we parted. He later called to say that he had sourced a field next to the pub in Little Hayfield (very helpful indeed). As we passed through Broad Bottom and passed under the railway viaduct, I then took a route that looked tempting on the map. This soon ended up becoming an impassable footpath and footbridge. A very tight U turn was needed and then Marv ripped his saddle bags getting out of the dell in which we had found ourselves. I was doubly annoyed by an incurred waste of time and by taking a path I probably knew at the time, was too tight for a horse. This was a repeat of an earlier mistake in the Borders with the same consequences. I still hadn't learnt. We continued on by road.

Marv keeps guard at Mottram while I buy us lunch

The day just got hotter and hotter, and the roads continued to be rolling, making our progress slow. Through Charlesworth, where Marv took a great drink out of an old trough, and then up to 379 metres on the Monks Road. We both were getting a bit too tired to appreciate the views, and I was grateful when we started our final descent down to the A624 to get out of the sun. We found the Lantern Pike pub and I went in to introduce myself. They were expecting us and we were shown round the back to a field adjacent to the pub beer garden. There had been a funeral that day of a popular local man who actually owned the field we were in. The wake was being held in the pub, and I was asked back later to join them for drinks. The departed gentleman's wife offered to fix my saddlebag and duly left to go back to her nearby house to get the sewing machine out. I put up my bivi in a sheltered corner of Marv's field and had some noodles and a well-earned siesta. The lovely lady came over later with the repaired saddle bag, and with my spirits lifted from the repair, I dropped into the pub to join the throng. They all were very interested in the trip and thought it fitting that I was here on this day. The departed gentleman was apparently very keen on horses and would have been proud to know that Marv and I had joined the wake. I went to bed that night in a very positive mood after meeting so many friendly and generous people, I was discovering that many people are intrinsically kind and helpful even to wandering strangers.

Day 40 (Little Hayfield to Blackwell - 23 miles)

We got up early, with a long day to complete, and walked down into Hayfield where we picked up the Pennine bridleway again, this time following the south side of the Peak District National Park. After a climb up to around 400m we contoured round the hills with an awesome view to the west. The bridleway was excellent here, and the miles flew by. This was ideal terrain and the going was much better for Marv. There were many gates to go through, but all were horse friendly. The bridleway passed through the small village of Peak Forest, where the Post Office was unfortunately shut. I was forced therefore to have lunch at the local pub instead.

As we had made good time I chose to have a relaxed lunch outside in the pub beer garden, with Marv patiently standing next to me at the picnic table. The pub owners were ok with this and offered him some apples and carrots. After lunch it was back on the bridleway for a steady section to reach the hamlet of Blackwell. It had been a long slog today and I asked at the first farm for a field to stay in. David of Crossroads Farm was very helpful, and in the paddock provided I pitched my bivi against a dry stone wall, whilst Marv set to work on the grass. I got into my sleeping bag hoping for a few hours rest, and was awoken not long after by a young girl on a pony, who asked about Marv. She promised to return later with some hard feed for Marv. Sure enough half an hour later, she was back with her mother with all sorts of goodies for Marv. Tonight I was not as lucky as Marv with my dinner, and I tucked into my noodle supper out of the mess tin.

Day 41 (Blackwell to Ashbourne - 20 miles)

Marv was my early alarm clock again, as he could smell the sugar beet mash that was left by the girl from last night. I gave Marv his breakfast and decided to get up anyway and make a start. Marv was so keen to eat his sugar beet that he broke the bucket in his eagerness to get to the bottom. I felt a bit guilty when we left, but there was little I could do but wash out the remains of the bucket. Marv also ended up with half his face covered in black beet after he got his nose wedged in the bucket, greedy boy! We set off in the mist, which cleared as we climbed up to bypass Chelmorton. Down the other side, the bridleway ran on a disused railway, which I relished for its speed and economy of effort.

Marv munching in the mist (on the Pennine bridleway)

David Boyd was the local ILPH officer for this area. He had been the Officer Commanding the riding school at Melton Mowbray when I went through training there. He had organised to meet me at the Waterloo public house at Biggin, just off the bridleway. I duly arrived at lunchtime, in the sun. There to meet us was David, and also a farrier from the King's Troop, Alex Mercer, who would change over a set of Marv's shoes during lunch. We sat outside having a wonderful pub lunch and catching up on the trip and the Army. We managed a photo by the pub sign, which showed Army horses and soldiers at Waterloo, very fitting I thought. After saying goodbye, we headed back onto the Pennine bridleway and old railway line for some more miles.

The scenery became a bit less dramatic as we left the Peak district behind, and I was glad to be approaching Ashbourne in Staffordshire. David had also spoken to the local Ashbourne newspaper and a lovely female reporter called Danielle met me just as the bridleway entered the town. She had sorted a field for Marv, and she led the way to John Stubb's farm. Danielle had ridden at this yard when she was younger and so knew them well. Once Marv was safely in his field for the night, I was offered the use of a shower and the farm caravan, which I gratefully accepted. Danielle came back later to pick me up and take me to her Dad's pub for some dinner.

I learnt from Danielle that Ashbourne had a long tradition of holding an annual match between the uppers and downers (two halves of the town). A huge number of the men of the town take part. To win, one side must get the 'ball' to the opponent's goal (the goals are 6 miles apart). This can take a whole day and is very physical competition, with few rules. Her dad had been a rare goal scorer in the past and the winning 'ball' was displayed in the pub. He was certainly a hard looking man....no messing with him. Danielle also wanted to meet me in the morning to get a photograph and ask some more questions for her article. Before turning in I went to check up on Marv, who was lying down by the gate, as close as he could get to a grey mare in the adjoining field, to whom I daresay he had formed an attachment.

Day 42 (Ashbourne to Kingstone - 23 miles)

I got up to feed Marv at 0630, but he was more interested in necking with the mare. We set off and met up with Danielle on the outskirts for the photo, with the town as the backdrop. She accompanied me for half an hour showing me one of the 'ball' goals as we passed. Soon after, on some quiet back roads, we passed Abbotsholme School, where many years ago I had competed in the National Independent Schools cross country championships, and then Rocester (for a sandwich). We then passed the huge JCB factory just north of Uttoxeter, which had its own lake and gardens. Marv had a big drink out of the lake alongside the resident ducks.

I decided that we ought to canter down the tree lined parkland, which woke Marv up. I then opted to go through the outskirts of Uttoxeter instead of skirting round, which saved a mile, but was not terribly scenic. We certainly preferred the quieter routes. We met a female police officer who was interested in long distance riding, and it was good to share experiences. We pushed on to the pub in Bramshall, where we stopped for some water for Marv. The locals all chipped in a fair sum for the charities, which was greatly appreciated. It was then only a short hop of 3 miles to the little village of Kingstone where a field had just been arranged (by Fi, that same day) for Marv. I put up my bivi in the field and then had my customary late afternoon kip, before heading to the nearby Shrewsbury Arms for my supper. Another week completed, and we were clear of the north, and heading into more familiar territory next week.

Day 43 (Kingstone - rest day)

Jill, who had kindly allowed the field for Marv, cooked me a superb breakfast and offered to do some washing for me. This was great news and my day off was greatly improved by her generosity. I also was allowed to charge my phone in the nearby barn, and being quite tired, I slept for 3 hours in the tack room whilst it charged. I went back up to the pub for my lunch, which they very kindly wouldn't accept payment for. The afternoon was spent chilling in the field in the sun with Marv. Jill very generously brought me a dinner out to the bivi with a bottle of beer. A good day off and well rested for the next push.

Week 7 (76 miles)

Week 7 (total 76 miles)

Day 44 (Kingstone to Codsall - 23 miles)

Having reviewed the next few days I changed my original route from here to Worcester to give Marv and myself the longer break I thought we both needed. I had planned to go further west initially and also stop at my friend James' family farm in Stottesdon, but that meant crossing the River Severn twice unnecessarily. So I missed out a planned stopover in Gnosall which made today longer but gained a rest day. The route today took me around the north edge of the huge conurbation of Birmingham, but just south of Stafford. Jill provided yet another superb cooked breakfast to see me out of Staffordshire. Sun cream was duly applied to Marv's pink nosey bits, much to his disgust. He still didn't understand that it was for his benefit.

I had not been going long before a gentleman in a 4x4 stopped and handed over a sizeable £40 donation. He didn't give his name, but I noticed he did work for (or own) Wickers World hot air balloon company. Many thanks sir.

It was a hot day and so we stopped for a break at Milford Common, Marv got his grass whilst I got 40 winks. Soon after, we crossed under the M6 motorway onto the Staffordshire & Worcestershire Canal path. As we went under the noisy concrete road bridge, I saw how two eras were transposed so differently. The tranquil (almost natural) canal waterway has been overpassed and overtaken by the seemingly aggressive and unstoppable road network. The sad fact is that when most of us use the motorways (me included) we miss so much of the finest parts of the country as we speed on by. Not so when travelling with a horse.

Staffs & Worcs Canal

Just the other side of the M6 and far enough away from the motorway to be peaceful once more, was the delightfully scenic village of Penkridge. I would imagine this is an ideal but expensive commuter settlement for people working in Birmingham, it having its own railway station on the west coast mainline. We were both very relaxed today, despite the long miles, as the route was flat and we made good speed. We crossed the very busy A5, and then from Brewood it was onto the Shropshire Union Canal for the last hour. Getting Marv down to the canal path was a challenge, as it was a long steep set of wooden steps, but Marv behaved like a mountain goat and willingly followed me down.

(L) Shropshire Union Canal, (R) Marv and friends at Upper Hattons

We managed a brisk trot into Upper Hattons, where we were booked in for the night. I had spent a raucous night here twenty years ago just after leaving school. It was in a school leavers' barn dance and house party when we were all 18. Tim, whose house it had been then, had put me in touch with the new owners and they had just bought a horse foot spa and wanted Marv to be the first horse to trial it before it was available to others. It sounded ideal for the weary equine traveller.

Sue met us as we arrived, and once I had un-tacked him, I led Marv straight into the equine foot spa room. He was certainly cautious about this, but having just travelled all day, he was much calmer than if it had been first thing in the morning. Once in the spa, the rear door of the box was closed up and the cold water spa was turned on. The theory is that a foot and a half of icy cold water, combined with jets of air through the water around your horse's feet will ease any swelling. Marv was surprised by the bubbles coming on and let loose with an impromptu huge horse poop, which was caught by a special bag attached to the rear for such an eventuality. Marv got a good half an hour in the spa, before being let out into a field for some peace and some well-earned grass. My very good school friend Pete drove up from nearby Ludlow and we nipped away for an Indian takeaway dinner and to catch up on news. It was also Pete's birthday so a special occasion for us to enjoy. Pete was later to pick us up at the finish. I spent an unfortunately restless night on the sofa, perhaps the bivi would have been a better option?

Day 45 (Codsall to Trimpley - 20 miles)

I was up early and away before the sun got too hot. We made a quick stop for a Cornish pasty and juice, before hitting some great bridleways (at last). It was called the Monarch's Way/Staffordshire Way, and at one point on it we were cantering through the middle of a mature wheat field which felt cool. We were then just passing a golf course, when the sprinklers were turned on. This spooked Marv and we raced ahead at double speed for a while until he calmed down and decided he was safe at last.

(L) Fantastic bridle path through wheat, (R) Marv admires a passing motorbike

I met James (from Stottesdon) near the village of Pattingham. James had taken a day off work to join me on his racing bike. We soon stopped for a picnic lunch which he had kindly brought, before I led us on a merry dance over ploughed fields trying to follow the indistinct bridleway. Once again the bridleway (signage and network, not my map reading...) had let me down, and we wasted an hour extricating a horse and bike rider with clip on shoes (carrying his bike) from several impenetrable barbed wired dead end fields with no gates. Once back on the minor roads we made up some time and I apologised for having tried the bridleways in the first place.

James and Marv before the speed test

As James had a cycle computer on his bike we decided to accurately measure the speed of Marv's trot. We discovered that Marv could do a maximum of 13mph if he wanted to. That was a very quick trot and not sustainable for long, but interesting to note all the same. We were now tracing the border with Shropshire (the county I went to school in), and I now started to feel like I was in familiar territory after covering totally new ground for the last two weeks. We made it down to Shatterford late afternoon, which took us into Worcestershire. James peeled off to cycle back home and Marv and I completed the last short hop to Trimpley.

We were met there by Barbara, Fi's mother, who lived in nearby Worcester. Barbara had managed to locate a field, courtesy of James and Ann, for Marv for the night. We went in to the field owner's house to say hello and meet their many dogs. Marv got his evening meal of muesli and we left him in good hands as we travelled to Worcester for the night. I was thankful for the relaxing pleasure of a bath and the knowledge that we had a few days off to unwind and take stock. Fi and Maisie arrived later after a long drive down from Edinburgh. It was great to catch up with them both, as we had seen them every weekend for the first four weekends, and it felt like the team was back together. In writing this now I can see how much time and incredible effort Fi put into the trip (at the same time as doing her normal job). Whilst I was heading south with Marv, she was continually keeping the diary up to date, uploading photos and driving hundreds of miles to meet up with us. I think at the time I was too focused on my route to really appreciate the full extent of her energies.

Day 46 (Trimpley to Martley - 16 miles)

This was a first for me and Fi, as she was able to walk with us for the full day, courtesy of Barbara, who dropped us off back at Trimpley. Marv was keen to go after his breakfast, and so we headed off with Maisie pleased to be back on the road too. The heavens opened for a short while, but soon after the waterproofs were taken off. We reached Bewdley, where we met local riders Anna and Rosemary who were keen to walk through town with us. As we were talking we discovered that Anna's daughter Katie had been at Pony club together with Fi many moons ago! Before they departed they left a kind donation to the ILPH.

We were now seeing road signs for Martley (our destination) and to celebrate we stopped in the village store of Great Witley for an ice cream. It turns out that Marv likes Strawberry Calypsos, to add to his list of unlikely equine tastes. We concluded the last few miles to Martley, where Sheila (a great family friend of Barbara and Fi) had a secluded farmstead. Marv had plenty company at Sheila's, with chickens and sheep all sharing his massive field. He even had a huge open shelter to use if it rained. We left him with another huge feed and in Sheila's capable care. Later on we headed to the local pub for some good food and wine and a proper catch up on the last few week's travels.

(L) Worcestershire red sandstone, (R) more bonding over food

Days 47/48/49 (Martley - rest days)

The decision to push on this week and get to Worcestershire ahead of schedule was a good one, and the long (three day) weekend off meant that we could visit James in Stottesdon for a barbeque, with Pete also joining us again. We also had a barbeque in Worcester, with my sister, Sarah who came up from London, and Army mate Kev from Birmingham. Sarah was able to go out to Martley with us and meet Marv when we checked up on him each day, to ensure he was doing ok and not feeling neglected.

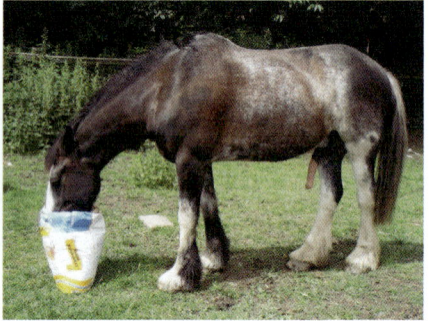

(Top) Maisie wants to play with James' cat, (L) Maisie tries bareback riding, (R) Marv enjoying the Staypower mix too much…

Day 50 (Martley to Worcester - 5 miles)

We took up the offer of Fi's uncle to move Marv into his garden in Worcester on Monday so that Tuesday's distance was reduced. We went out to Martley in the afternoon and Barbara dropped Fi, Maisie and me off. We only had a few miles to cover, and Fi knew the route well as she had ridden there as a youngster. To give Marv a break we had no saddle or saddlebags. I suggested Fi canter Marv bareback across Broadheath Common, where she had ridden many years previously. It was a special moment for both of us. Once we got to Uncle Michael's house we led Marv onto the pristine lawn at the back of the house. We had warned that Marv might make a mess of the flower beds etc, and that risk was acknowledged. The first thing that Marv did on being let loose was head over to an overhanging tree and his head suddenly disappeared. There was a loud snap, as Marv had grabbed a large branch and ripped it off for a good munch. At that point we said good luck to Fi's uncle and aunt, and left them to watch Marv eat their garden.

(L) Fi canters Marv over Broadheath Common, (R) Marv disguised as a tree in Michael's garden

Week 8 (62 miles)

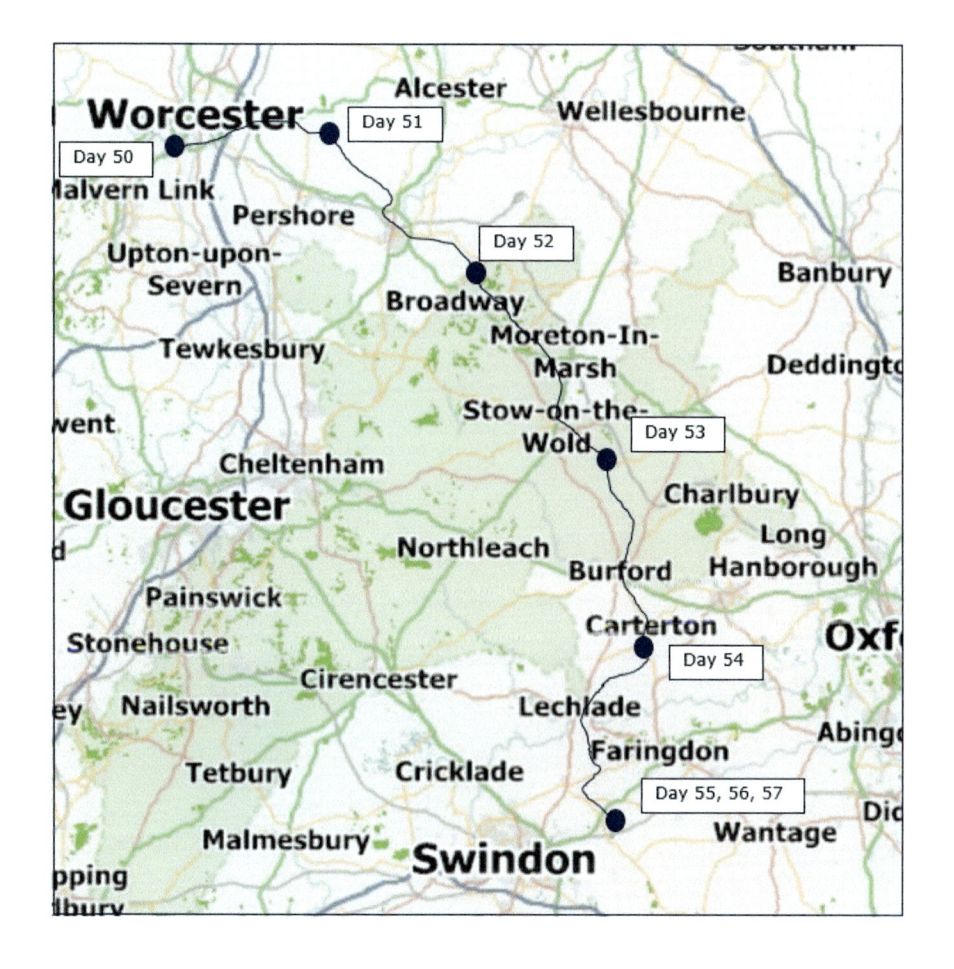

Week 8 (total 62 miles)

Day 51 (Worcester to Radford - 12 miles)

Marv had a great long weekend and had put on some weight in the girth area, which we would soon work off. We had a relaxed mid-morning start, then Fi and Maisie walked with us over the River Severn, through the centre of Worcester and crossed a bridge over the M5 motorway. A few miles further and we stopped as arranged at the Chequers Inn at Crowle. Marv was allowed an area for grazing, which we all helped cordon off, and then we trooped in (with Fi's mum, uncle and aunt) for a send-off lunch. Fi and the Mooch would then head back north and I would continue on with Marv. After saying my farewells, I headed east and found some great bridleways, getting Marv back in the swing with some fast canters. It was mid-afternoon when I reached my next destination, a friend's house in Radford. Emma was a keen horsewoman herself and kept numerous competition horses. We got Marv settled in a field, then caught up on our news. After dinner, as it looked like raining, we brought him in for a dry night's rest in a comfy stable.

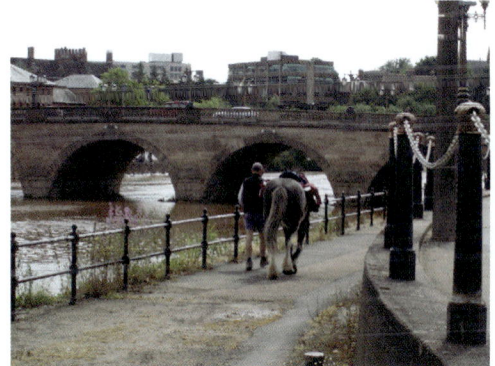

(L) Just about to cross the River Severn at Worcester, (R) window shopping

Day 52 (Radford to Weston sub Edge - 16 miles)

We were up quite early, and left at 0900. Marv was keen to keep moving and set a good pace. My intended route today crossed the River Avon at Harvington, but there had been some heavy rainfall recently and I was told by a local postmaster that the ford was too dangerous to use. I therefore had to divert south through Evesham. It was not the most scenic of detours, but it was fun riding and leading through the town centre. We then crossed a bridge which shortly after (the next day actually) was impassable due to flooding. We escaped just ahead of some of the worst flooding to hit this part of England for decades.

(L) Marv crossing the River Avon at Evesham, (R) following me through the pedestrianised zone

We passed through a delightful hamlet called Bretforton before concluding the day's travels at Weston Sub Edge. Here I had been extremely lucky in that a kind gentleman called William Reddaway had paid for a horse B&B for us. William was hoping to do a similar ride taking in all of England's Cathedrals in 5 years' time, when he retired. He was keen to meet me and discuss logistics and preparation. Lucy of Manor Farm (a 17th century Cotswold farmhouse) provided an incredible one bedroom apartment for me, and Marv got his luxury stable. We then joined the family and William for a sumptuous dinner and wine in the farmhouse before William and I spent some time going over his necessary preparations for his forthcoming trip. William has recently completed the trip of 2500 miles round England taking in 30 Cathedrals, a very impressive feat.

Day 53 (Weston sub Edge to Bledington - (16 miles)

I was treated to an amazing cooked breakfast by Lucy, and we then headed off south. We were now in the Cotswolds in the wealthy county of Gloucestershire, and the houses were certainly the smartest I'd seen on my travels so far. The start of the day was a sharp climb up to Chipping Campden, a classic Cotswold village, which looked unchanged from centuries past. Onwards took me to Moreton in Marsh, where I picnicked in the square watching the slow bustle of people going about their business. No-one was in the least fussed by Marv grazing on the verge at the centre of the village.

Marv in Chipping Camden and Moreton in Marsh

Our next pit stop was a roadside rendezvous with Charlie the local farrier, who managed to track me down and who re shod Marv in a lay by. This was prearranged and we hoped this would be the last pair of shoes needed until the end.

Pit stop in a layby for new front shoes

The last few miles today were not as picturesque as the morning, but we found Pebble Hill Stud just outside Bledington and I introduced myself. I had managed to secure a stable here for Marv through a former girlfriend of mine Sally, who worked there as a professional dressage groom. She was away on holiday, but her boss Jackie had said we could stay. The setup was high quality, and Marv received a huge box and feed to match. I was given keys to Sally's flat above the stables and from it you could watch all the horses in their boxes through internal windows. It was ideal to keep a check on Marv. After a shower, Jackie and her boyfriend very kindly took me out to supper at a local popular Cotswold hostelry.

Day 54 (Bledington to Carterton - 14 miles)

The rain finally caught up with us, and it was on with the waterproofs soon after the off. We passed through Shipton under Wychwood and I grabbed some food for the both of us from the Post Office there. After lunch, I was heading into familiar territory again, as I had lived at Carterton three times in my life when my late father was posted to the Parachute Training School at RAF Brize Norton. So for 9 years this had been my home. I started to recognise the area as we approached Swinbrook. My father used to canoe here regularly (when I was young) to practice his slalom turns on a course of poles built by the weir next to the pub on the River Windrush. I had this poignant memory in mind when we passed the same spot 30 years later. No slalom gates now, but the weir and pool on the Windrush were still the same

A couple of miles further, and after crossing the busy A40, we reached Carterton (which is probably the least attractive town anywhere in the Cotswolds). It has grown massively due to the expansion of the nearby RAF base. It seems that half the town is made up of nasty pre-fabricated boxes serving as married quarters for RAF families. We had stayed in three of these quarters during our time there. I was to be staying in another one tonight, courtesy of my Army friend Chris and his wife Nicky.

(L) Stuck at the gate, (R) saying hello though the kitchen window

Nicky was a navigator on VC10s at RAF Brize Norton, and so they lived in a married quarter together. Their house was identical to the ones we had lived in, so it was a bit surreal going back there. Marv was to be located in the back garden for the night. Unfortunately, Chris had just cut the grass, so we took Marv out to a local play area and let him loose so he could get an hour of proper grazing. Chris and I kept an eye on him and caught up over a gin & tonic. Once back in the garden, we opened the kitchen window and Marv spent the next hour with his head inside the house as we continued to catch up. All the local RAF kids had heard that Chris and Nicky had a horse in their garden and came to see Marv. Marv then came down the tight walkway by the side of the house and garage and stood at the side gate to see the kids out the front. However, he was then stuck and couldn't reverse to the back garden, so I led him out and turned him round.

Day 55 (Carterton to Shrivenham - 16 miles)

First thing in the morning we all rushed out to count how many poos Marv had done in their garden, as we had all guessed the number over dinner the evening before and Chris won with nine. We said our farewells and headed off out of town, on another familiar road, which in the past I had completed training runs on. The hamlets were still very pretty; Kencot, Langford and then the outskirts of Lechlade on Thames. Lechlade is almost the source of the River Thames, and a few years ago where I had started a trip to canoe the length of the Thames with Army mate Jody (a Gurkha officer). We only managed two days with one night's bivi out, before bailing out at Oxford as our double canoe was taking on water.......something we may return to and complete one day.

Marv inspects a herd of curious cows

After Lechlade it was a fairly flat and easy distance over to Watchfield, the village adjacent to the Royal Military College of Science (RMCS) at Shrivenham. Here we had a field organised for Marv courtesy of my good friend Dave. He was one of the colleagues who I had been riding with at Larkhill in our young Gunner officer training days. He was now a Major and was on his Staff officer's course at the RMCS. As it was the weekend, he had kindly organised for me to use his room in the College. Dave had also promised to be there to meet me for the weekend, but alas on this occasion, Dave's social life in London took priority.

I managed to get in the main gate of the camp, and found the field that the saddle club had organised. The camp was deserted, as all the military students head off at the weekends. After getting Marv sorted, I went off to find Dave's room, and I thought that this might be a bit of a quiet weekend being here on my own. I got on the phone and called Army mate Matt who lived at nearby Upavon, and who I had booked in to stay with early next week. Matt was incredible. He would not hear of me staying at RMCS on my own, and drove up immediately to collect me. We spent half an hour picking ragwort from the field first, as I was paranoid about Marv not getting ill. Then it was back to his large married quarter to stay with his wife Fee and son Freddie for the weekend. It was such a welcome surprise to have Matt and his family for company and to be looked after so well.

Day 56 (Shrivenham - rest day)

Through my limited press coverage, Marv's adventure came to the attention of Pippa Winkworth, who was an equine physiotherapist. She lived in Sussex I think, and she had agreed to drive up to Shrivenham to give Marv a free back massage. Amazing! Matt drove me back up to Shrivenham, and then Pippa turned up after her long drive, and gave Marv an hour of rigorous equine sports massage treatment. Pippa commented afterwards that she was amazed how healthy and relaxed his back was after the many hundreds of miles. I thanked her profusely for the treatment, and was comforted in the knowledge that Marv's back was sound. Pippa had just started her own business and was keen to use Marv's treatment as a PR story, which I thought a great idea.

After Marv's equine massage at Shrivenham

Day 57 (Shrivenham - rest day)

Today was a fully relaxing one with the Sunday papers, and eating great food. I managed to do some trip admin and catch up with my diary for the week. It was great to be able to spend quality time with Matt and Fee and a very enjoyable weekend was had.

Enjoying his rest day too

Week 9 (64 miles)

Week 9 (total 64 miles)

Day 58 (Shrivenham to Marlborough - 16 miles)

We left Upavon early to drop Freddie at Nursery and then Matt dropped me back at RMCS. It was raining hard and the outlook didn't suggest an improvement. We had stopped at the Co-op for carrots and apples to raise Marv's damp spirits. Matt fed Marv under a tree for shelter, whilst I saddled him up. We were both cold and so as soon as we left camp I started running to warm us up. In full waterproofs this occurred quite quickly, and within a mile I had to take the leggings off. First stop was the local Post Office to send back my photo sim card and diary to Fi. A very considerate lady who had chatted to me in the Post Office then bought me a hot sausage roll with coffee and a snack for Marv. This was great for morale.

Off we trotted down the back lanes of Wiltshire and crossed over the M4 motorway. The rain held off and we utilised the scenic route of the Old Ridgeway, which led into the Marlborough Downs as we passed by Barbury Castle racecourse. The surrounding views were well worth the climb. It was clear that we were now entering prime real estate, as all around us were immaculate fields, smart fencing, tree lined avenues and numerous gallops for training racehorses. Inspired by the equine theme I pushed Marv on with some long canters down the well maintained grass verges, pretending that we too were part of the racehorse fraternity.

(L) Crossing the M4, (C) view towards Marlborough, (R) near Barbury Castle

A delightful meandering lane led us down to Temple Farm, nestled in its own private valley. If I recall correctly, Dave (whilst at RMCS) had managed to speak to fellow army officer Melissa at Shrivenham (as she was on his course). Melissa was into horses and knew Susie of Temple Farm, who kindly offered a stable for Marv. I was met by Sarah, Susie's head groom, who offered a roomy stable and also the use of a field. She had a Parson Russell terrier, who I played with for at least half an hour, missing Maisie's antics. I put Marv out for a while to get him some good grazing, before the heavens opened and I quickly moved him indoors for a drier evening. I was met by a friend Nicola, who had driven up from Reading with her boyfriend, to meet Marv. They took me out for dinner in Marlborough to hear about the trip and then dropped me back at Upavon.

Day 59 (Marlborough to Larkhill - 22 miles)

Today, it was Fee who took me to Temple Farm with Freddie to start the day off. Marv and I headed out of Temple Bottom and up onto the Wessex Ridgeway, which doubled as a local gallop for Manton (a huge race yard once owned by Robert Sangster). We trooped down into the historic town of Marlborough and sauntered through with no one taking much notice, as they must be so used to horses in the area. Out the other side, it was a steep climb and a few miles on we reached a viewpoint where I could see stretched out before me the wide expanse of Salisbury Plain. This was a military training area I had spent some time on, and even today the Artillery were live firing, as I could hear the guns and see the shells exploding on the impact area in the distance. It was good to be back, and not in uniform.

I would be meeting up today with my good friend, and house mate from University, Heath. Heath had gone to Marlborough School and knew the area well, so it was fitting that he would be joining me today especially. He had driven down from Oxford, and we met at the pub at Wilcot, where he left his car, and we carried on with him in his running kit. Today was a relatively long day so we pushed on with the pace. This had to be interrupted by the obligatory pub lunch at Woodbridge on the A345. I got permission from the landlord to let Marv graze in the pub beer garden whilst Heath and I had a quick pint and food outside at a picnic table.

Heath has always been afraid of horses, and he slowly became more confident being around Marv. Soon after lunch I convinced him to have a short sit on Marv. Heath is 6ft 4" and 15 stone, and I could just imagine Marv's thinking "you must be joking!" as I legged Heath up. Heath lasted only five seconds, as the girth was too loose. I ran back to catch Heath as he was swinging round Marv's belly but still clinging on. A second attempt was more successful, and after Heath had broken his fear of horses, I remounted and we continued down the charming Avon valley on a minor road past numerous thatched cottages.

(L) Heath briefly rides Marv, (R) pit stop for a pint

We came very close to Matt's married quarter at Upavon and then through East Chisenbury and Longstreet, where we gave in again to the delights of the country pub for another shandy. At Netheravon, we crossed the river and main road to travel on the training area itself. By using the range road we approached Larkhill camp along the familiar dusty chalk tracks. Larkhill is the home of the Royal Artillery and where I really started to learn to ride. This felt a bit like a pilgrimage, going back to where it all began. We circled around the perimeter of the camp and entered by the main gate. Yet again, I had mixed feelings being back. This had been my home back in 1998, but I was no longer in the Royal Artillery yet still felt a very strong connection.

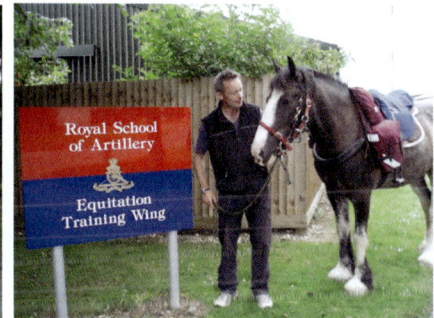

Where my love of riding really began – Royal School of Artillery stables, Larkhill

We arrived at the RA stables on camp, and said hello to Sgt Taff Jeffries (of the King's Troop) who was in charge of the stables. He was one of the Gun No.1s who had been with me at the Edinburgh Tattoo. We were shown Marv's stable by two other soldiers who had been in Centre Section with me (Ben Moore and 'Grandma' Illingworth). Matt joined us after work, still in his uniform and we had a few photographs taken around Larkhill for Gunner magazine. Matt drove Heath back to his car and then we returned to Upavon for supper and an early night. This was easily one of the best days of the trip by far.

Day 60 (Larkhill to Fovant - 14 miles)

Matt dropped me off early back at Larkhill, before heading off to Wilton and work. I am deeply indebted to both Matt and Fee for being so incredible this week and going out of their way to accommodate me and Marv as we passed through the area. I fed and mucked out Marv, who had clearly been gonking (military term for sleeping) heavily, judging by the amount of shavings he was wearing when I arrived. As today was a short one, Taff and I caught up on King's Troop news in his office and then we took some pictures in front of the Officer's Mess which I will always treasure. We headed out the main gate and after a quick shop stop we took the track to Stonehenge.

(L) In front of the Officers Mess at Larkhill, (R) Marv gazes on Stonehenge

Previously, when the King's Troop was temporarily based up at Larkhill for a show, I had been out hacking alone on one charger with another in hand. It was at this location, on a track near Stonehenge that I had decided that cantering the two horses would be ok, as the track was in the middle of nowhere and was quite straight. However the two horses started racing and we were soon galloping along with no easy way of stopping. The busy A303 road was fast approaching and I did just manage to bring them back to a walk in time. I have no regrets over the incident as it was very exciting at the time.

This time though with Marv it was much more sedate. I had a rendezvous with another Army mate Jody. Jody had been in my Platoon at Sandhurst, he was a career soldier and probably should have won the Sword of Honour. He joined the Gurkhas, is very keen and green and may yet one day reach the rank of General. Jody met up with me at Great Wishford. Jody was in his running kit too, and had cycled over on his lunch break from nearby Wilton, to join me for a few miles and a pub lunch.

Some quick miles and lunch with Jody at Dinton

It was great to catch up again and we made good time, as Jody also needed to do some training for a forthcoming 100km race on the South Downs. We had an outdoor lunch at Dinton, with Marv doing his customary graze about the beer garden. After the obligatory photo call, Jody ran the 10km back to his bike and I carried on the few remaining miles to Fovant.

Once at the village, I soon found Neil's house. When Ellie (Neil's wife) opened the front door Marv started to walk in to the house thinking that maybe it was his home for the night. We backed Marv up a bit and dropped off his saddle and bags, before walking him through the village to a local livery yard owned by Linda. Linda took great care of Marv for his two night stay in Fovant.

Neil was another Army mate, with whom I had survived Rowallan Company, then the Commissioning Course and finally the RA Young Officers' course at RSA Larkhill together. I also joined Neil at the King's Troop, as he had been posted there a year before me. Neil arrived straight from work in his uniform, and we thereafter spent the evening catching up. Neil showed me his two pigs which he had recently bought to go with his four chickens and two geese in his garden. Very Hugh Fearnley-Whittingstall…. and they do look oddly similar too?

Day 61 (Fovant - day off to meet the Queen)

Today we (Neil, Ellie and I) were off to see the 60th anniversary of the King's Troop parade which was being held in Hyde Park, London. Neil lent me the requisite suit and tie, and we drove to Twickenham, where we then caught a train into central London. We had lunch with Mike who was the vet when we were both serving with the King's Troop, before walking over to take our positions adjacent to Park Lane. Major Erica Bridge led the King's Troop parade which included a canter past in front of the Queen. Erica was the Adjutant when Neil and I were at the Troop. After the parade it was into the marquee for tea and sandwiches with members of the Troop, ex Troop officers and the Queen, before heading back to Fovant after a memorable day. It was very fortuitous that I had been at Fovant at this particular time to enable the London visit to happen. Marv benefited from an extra day off mid-week, and it was great to catch up with friends in London mid trip.

(L) The King's Troop RHA parades for the Queen in Hyde Park, (R) drinks afterwards with Rob (fellow Troop officer) and HRH

Day 62 (Fovant to Shaftesbury - 12 miles)

I got up early to say goodbye and thanks to Neil as he left for work, before going back to bed to catch up on my diary. I didn't have many miles to do today, and it was raining, and so no rush to leave. Ellie made me a superb breakfast with their own free range eggs. Les from Free N' Easy arrived for my second en route saddle check. We headed round the corner to see Linda, and Les made some minor adjustments on Marv's saddle. It was good to see Les again, who was down in the south west doing his regular customer care round trip.

(L) At the front door of Neil & Ellie's house in Fovant, (R) at Gear's Mill

As my rendezvous tonight was not to be before 1700, I stayed around to have a surprise lunch with Neil again. After another great spread I nipped back to the yard to collect Marv. I returned on him bareback to collect his saddle and bags. He was fresh and certainly on his toes. So much so, that when Ellie was holding him whilst I loaded him up, he accidentally knocked her over and stood on her foot! Not a great way to say goodbye to such fantastic hosts. Marv was also so impatient to get going he broke his reins whilst tied up. I could see that Marv needed some work to settle him down again. His fitness was apparent and he wasn't doing well being overly rested.

We didn't get off until 1430, my latest start yet by far. I cantered him quite hard very early on, but had to get off to find a way through a high thorny hedge line, and we had to spend ten minutes battling our way through the hedge (with saddlebags removed). Finally we reached the ridgeline of the South Downs, and we turned west and managed a monster trot along the puddle infested byway. We had to drop down to the busy A30 for 800 metres, before turning off and following minor roads the last few miles into Shaftesbury and Dorset. I would be staying at Gear's Mill with Commodore Richard Bridges and his daughter Lucy. A few years ago I had been living for a few months nearby in Wiltshire, and had the privilege to ride out a few times for Mrs Bridges, a successful race horse trainer with a small yard. I was met by Lucy and she found Marv a great field. Later on, Richard took me to a great local pub, the Foresters, for a superb meal and engaging conversation.

Day 63 (Shaftesbury to Purse Caundle - 14 miles)

Richard had left early to go sailing on the Solent, so I moved Marv into a stable at 0800 to help dry him before we set off. We left at 1030, after having a chat with Lucy and waiting for the rain to ease. I rode Marv out the yard and up the steep slippery bridleway above Gear's Mill to get a mobile signal. Once linked to the mobile network I was able to make contact with University friend Nick, who I had shared a student house with for two years. Nick lived in Henley on Thames, and therefore had quite a drive to join me as I headed deeper into Dorset.

We met up with each other next to HM prison at Guy's March, where he left his car and joined me in his slightly pesty (too tight) rowing lycra. Again, it was good to catch up on the hoof, and we made our way across country to have lunch at the Crown in Marnhull. The weather wasn't with us today, and we had to sit out in the drizzle as Marv ignored the rain and munched on. We started to see signs of the exceptionally wet weather Britain had been experiencing this year. Later, at one point we found the road was totally flooded ahead. I was fine sitting high on Marv, but Nick had his trainers and Ronhill leggings to think of. By using his initiative, he managed to hitch a lift (not sure how, in his outfit) with a lady driver for 100 metres through the flooded section just to keep his gear dry.

(L) Nick meets Marv, (C) riding the flooded lane, (R) last mile into Purse Caundle

We passed through Stalbridge and finally onto a hill overlooking Purse Caundle. It had just rained quite hard, but we needed to take a photo regardless, to capture the day. Finally we got the required photo and slipped our way down a steep path and into the village. We were met at Home Farm by Judy, Anthony and Amelia. These were Fi's relations and they were hugely welcoming to me and Marv. Marv was loosed out into a field to share with a herd of dairy cows and their own horse Geoffrey (who had his own electric fence enclosure in the cow's field), whilst we conversed in the kitchen by the Aga to warm up. Antony very kindly offered to drive Nick back to his car, and I said farewell to one of the many close friends who I had the privilege to meet up with, and share a memorable part of the trip with this week. Back at Home Farm I was treated to a huge beef casserole and glad to be inside as the weather was not looking favourable.

Day 64 (Purse Caundle - day off)

I was up at 0800 for breakfast with the family. I then joined them in moving the dairy herd from one field to another some distance away. Soon after, the first of today's visitors was Caroline (a University friend, whom I mentioned earlier, and had inspired me to be a better rider). She was en route with her husband Charlie and young son William to go on holiday to Cornwall, and had detoured to come and meet Marv. She couldn't stay long, but it meant a great deal that she went out of her way to catch up with us. As Caroline arrived, Amelia returned from hacking out on Geoffrey. He was then released into the field with Marv, whereby they both behaved like big kids, chasing each other round the field, breaking the electric fence, but having a huge amount of fun in the process. This was meant to be Marv's rest day, but clearly he had far too much energy still. I was just glad that that they got on, and Marv was able to spend some down time with another horse. It must be difficult for a herd animal to spend the night somewhere different each day, often with no other horses for company. During the whole trip, if we ever met horses in fields as we passed I would always take the time to stop and let Marv meet the horses. It would usually involve some mutual nose sniffing and then a squeal from the other horse, with Marv then snorting and abruptly turning to continue on our way. Back in the field, Marv and Geoffrey did calm down and then spent the next hour mutually grooming each other.

Marv and Geoffrey necking

We had a pause for a ploughman's lunch, before friends of my parents from the RAF days, Linda and Roger, came to feed Marv some more treats. They were closely followed by Susan and Patrick who had heard about the trip and had driven up from Bridport to meet Marv too. I spent the later part of the afternoon trying to organise fields for the last two weeks of the trip (through Devon and Cornwall) which I had purposely left unplanned to add some adventure to the finish. My initial planning had me stopping in villages which had a PH (public house) on the map. My thought process was at least if there was a pub I could get a meal on arrival. Taking that one step further, I used the internet to find out the pub's names and numbers, and then called them all up, explaining my trip and asking nicely for potential fields for Marv. It was instantly successful, with many pubs sorting the field request on the spot, with others calling me back later after speaking to the locals.

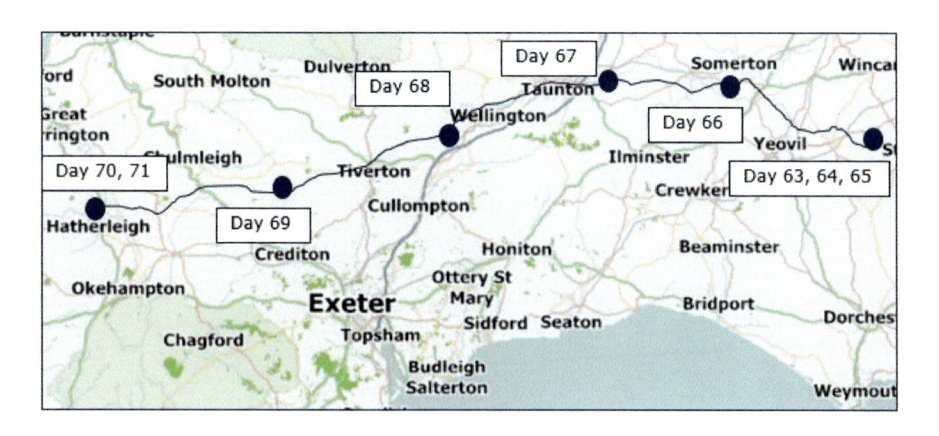

Week 10 (89 miles)

Week 10 (total 89 miles)

Day 65 (Purse Caundle - extra rest day)

Today was a bonus rest day, awarded to myself as I had deliberately left the last few weeks of the trip requiring less average miles in case I needed any extra time towards the end. After another superb cooked breakfast, I spent the best part of the morning catching up on diary writing, and then in the afternoon, time for a power nap and a nip down to the local Post Office to post the diary notes, used maps and photos back to Fi. I owe a big thanks to Home Farm for looking after me for the long weekend, and putting up with a stream of unexpected visitors on the Sunday.

Marv & Geoffrey's paddock

Day 66 (Purse Caundle to Somerton - 17 miles)

Tuesday started early, and after a quicker than normal breakfast, Amelia and I headed out to tack up the horses. Amelia was effectively the only person to join me on horseback for the trip. Geoffrey and Marv were now best friends having had a few days in the same field. The concern was how would Marv react when Geoffrey headed back to Home Farm? Amelia and I set off on some great tracks and soon we were at Milborne Port, where I stopped to buy some horse snacks and Amelia then turned back. Marv did his usual whinnying for a short while, but probably realised that we must just carry on.

(L) Amelia riding Geoffrey with us to Milborne Port, (R) posing at an impressive entrance

We stopped for a photo opportunity outside the manor house in the picturesque village of Sanford Orcas. It was then on through Marston Magna (another great name) before passing to the north of the Royal Naval Air Station (RNAS) at Yeovilton. We were treated to a free air show as numerous planes and helicopters were busy in the sky around us. Marv was not the least bit fussed by the noise of the aircraft. What did upset Marv was the bright orange airfield windsock which was flapping high above the perimeter fence next to us. Marv did his usual side stepping routine with his head held high, eyeballs popping, and much snorting. After we had escaped the wind sock 'monster' the heavens opened up and as Marv had no waterproofs we took respite in a bus shelter until the worst of the rain had fallen.

A little later on we reached Lyles Cary where we were met by two members of the ILPH team from their Somerton farm. They escorted us the last few miles to Glenda Spooner Farm. It so happened that the ILPH were having an equine documentary being filmed there (called 'Horse Patrol'), and they wanted to include some footage of our adventure. They filmed us from the back of a vehicle all the way into the farm, and so I had to put on my high-vis vest and helmet (which I had carried the whole way but rarely used). Once we reached the large ILPH facility, and the filming had been completed, Marv was let loose in the field and took the opportunity to do a series of rolls. The staff were surprised at how agile he was for a heavy horse breed. As Fi aptly acknowledged in the diary; "it is a pleasure to watch him as he nonchalantly sniffs around for the right spot before the knees buckle and he is down, grunting and groaning as he throws himself enthusiastically from side to side". Graham, an RAF friend of my parents, arrived and we headed down to the local pub to catch up for an hour, before heading back to the farm and sitting down for supper with the centre manager Janet and Andy.

Day 67 (Somerton to Creech St Michael - 18 miles)

First thing in the morning we led Marv onto the centre's weighbridge, and he tipped the scales at 628kg, which was quite trim apparently for a heavy horse. After the weigh in we departed the farm and headed off up the busy B3151 towards Somerton. We stopped at the local supermarket for our daily supplies and then Marv was fed some liquorice allsorts by a well-wisher. His tastes have certainly expanded whilst on the trip. Next destination was Langport, to cross the local river Yeo. The weather was turning wet again and I had to resort to using mint imperials as incentives for Marv to keep him moving at a healthy pace. After passing through Stoke St Gregory, North Curry and by the side of West Sedge Moor we reached Creech St Michael, our destination for today. I located Wendy at the local pub, who had a field organised for Marv. The field was fine, but it was the other side of the river to the local abattoir, which made me feel slightly uncomfortable. My cousin Collette and her husband Mark arrived soon after, and we left Marv grazing to head back to their house near Taunton. I welcomed the opportunity of a shower, before heading out and having our evening meal in the pub at Creech St Michael to keep an eye on Marv.

Verge grazing down the lanes

Day 68 (Creech St Michael to Holcombe Rogus - 18 miles)

After another hearty breakfast, I was driven back to Marv, and we carried on west passing under the M5 motorway alongside the Bridgwater and Taunton Canal, and into Taunton town centre. We didn't usually go through urban areas, but to bypass it meant adding more miles. We skirted past the local rugby club and then back out into the open country which is where we both preferred to be. The scenery here was especially pleasant, and traversing the lanes west of Taunton (following the route of the River Tone to the north of Wellington) was enjoyable.

(L) No verges here... (R) any grass will do

The rain started after lunch, and so despite the scenery, neither of us was too keen to hang around, but wanted to get to the next night stop location. I had failed to put on my waterproof trousers, and as a consequence was suffering from sodden legs. Just to make the day more interesting, we found ourselves passing a large pig farm. Marv's eyes were out on stalks and I instantly mounted and we did the fastest two mile trot of the trip, until Marv was sure that the fields alongside no longer had any pink occupants in them. We duly reached Holcombe Rogus slightly quicker as a result, and I managed to secure a night in a barn for Marv courtesy of Henry the local farmer. As Mark and Collete would not be picking me up until after their work, Henry offered me some of his homebrewed cider. It was more like Scrumpy Jack than Strongbow and just as potent. I was soon feeling the effects of the drink when I was found by Collete in the farmer's kitchen stuck in a comfy chair by the Aga. Mark and Collette very kindly drove me back to theirs for another comfy night.

Day 69 (Holcombe Rogus to Black Dog - 18 miles)

Once again, Mark and Collette drove me out to my start point to pick up Marv. We drove via David Pipe's nearby horse racing yard at Pond House, as I had once had the privilege of riding out with David in Shaftesbury and was keen to see where he trained. Mark, Collete and their dog were keen to walk with me for an hour, and it made a pleasant change to doing the miles with only Marv for company. It transpired that they liked the village of Holcombe Rogus so much (they had not been before) that they shortly afterwards bought a cottage there, and are still living there.

(L) King's College Taunton, (R) leafy tree kebab on the go

It was a dry and windy day, but thankfully no rain. After crossing the River Exe near Tiverton we came across the notorious rollercoaster hills which are well known to End to End cyclists who think that they are very close to the finish, only to be taken by surprise when they find the frequent steep gradients in the south west. We passed through Pennymoor and Puddington to reach the remote hamlet of Black Dog (quite a bleak place) and a slightly sinister name. I had not managed to secure a field here in advance, but I finally managed to find a friendly local called Ivor, who allowed me the use of his field for both Marv and me. I had not slept out for some days thanks to continued hospitality, and I selected an old metal roller to pitch my bivi next to. I headed to the Black Dog pub for supper whilst Marv busied himself with unlimited grass. The landlady was superb, and on leaving gave me a unique boil in the bag cooked breakfast, which only needed heating through for the next day. That, a packed lunch and donation, easily made up for the uncomfortable night's sleep I had due to the ground next to the roller being far from level.

Bivi at Black Dog

Day 70 (Black Dog to Hatherleigh - 19 miles)

Saturday morning was also dry, and I was keen to get moving after eating the best cooked breakfast under canvas. Marv bumbled up to me as I finished off packing and stood still waiting to be tacked up. He knew the mission and it was great to not have to go off and round him up every day. We pit stopped at the quaint local Post Office at Morchard Bishop, where I think I got a great photo of us both outside. Armed with mints and apples for Marv we were well set for a longish hilly day. We cracked on westwards down many a winding lane with Dartmoor only a few miles to our south.

I had a few flashbacks to my short time spent on Dartmoor during my Sandhurst days. We had spent a week criss-crossing it with bergens and carrying heavy ammunition cases. It was very unpleasant at the time, but character building stuff apparently. I was glad to be back in the area of my own accord and in a much more relaxing manner.

We stopped for lunch on a really quiet lane, and as Marv had been behaving so well, I took off his bridle and head collar to give him a chance to really take in some grass. I was lying back on the verge daydreaming, when around the corner came a combine harvester. There was no way to get to Marv in time, and he was cantering off down the lane away from the machine. I sprang up, grabbed the head collar and ran after him. Luckily the combine driver stopped and switched the engine off, which helped, as Marv did stop after 100 metres. I got him back under control and then led him into a field as the combine came past. It could have been worse, but I saw the funny side afterwards.

(L) Wading through the flooded lanes, (R) our shadow casts an eerie look

Back on track we pushed on to Monkokehampton to seek out a shop, but no luck. We therefore continued the last few miles to Hatherleigh and the end of week ten. Just before entering the village, we came across a flooded lane. It must have been a foot deep and with the central section having tall grass it looked a bit like a paddy field. Marv was well used to crossing water now, and as we walked through Marv also managed to somehow walk and drink at the same time. It was quite a remarkable feat and made me laugh out loud. We met up with Roger and Sue who owned a farm in Hatherleigh and who had previously offered a field for Marv. Marv was to share the field with two mares and some cows. He was very happy with this and was left to commence socialising with the others whilst I was offered a room in their adjacent farmhouse. Roger and Sue were very kind to me as I was scheduled to have a rest day on Sunday, and they were adamant that it was fine to stay with them for two nights. I was mightily relieved, as I had not slept well the night before and to have a rest day off in a house rather than under the bivi was a real bonus.

Day 71 (Hatherleigh - rest day)

Marv and I both needed this rest day as the miles had started to increase again after the luxury of a few shorter weeks, and the hills were certainly taxing. I spent the morning trying to sort out week eleven fields for Marv, and in the afternoon I was picked up by my cousin Brett (Collete's brother) and his young son Luke. We utilised the local hostelry and had lunch at the George Hotel in Hatherleigh. There was quite some time to catch up on as I had not seen Brett since his wedding ten years earlier. After lunch it was back to the farmhouse to watch the Wimbledon men's final....another bonus! I headed to bed early after supper to contemplate the last full week ahead of us.

(L) With Luke in Hatherleigh, (R) grazing at the farm in Hatherleigh

Week 11 (86 miles)

Week 11 (total 86 Miles)

Day 72 (Hatherleigh to Lifton/Launceston - 20miles)

The final full week started as usual with an early (full) breakfast. I brought Marv in and put him in a stable as it was still raining, and the skies had no intention of lightening up. I tacked Marv up under cover and then headed off towards Lifton with a generous packed lunch and with all my waterproofs on. Sue kindly took my week 10 diary notes and photo memory card to the Post Office for sending back to Fi.

Marv and I headed first into the scenic Hatherleigh town again to visit the Co-op for our daily supplies. A few hours later, we stopped at a fantastic village pub in Bratton Clovelly for a drink and to finally peel off the waterproofs. Two friendly fishermen from Birmingham generously donated money during the pit stop. Crossing the A30 we briefly stopped to let Marv meet some ponies in a nearby field. It transpired that one was a stallion pony and was going crazy with jealousy with Marv who was freely socialising with his harem. The stallion pony would chase each offending mare around the field after it had neared Marv. We quickly moved on

(L) Outside the pub in Bratton Clovelly, (R) yet more verge munching

We arrived in Lifton in good time at 1600, after finishing on a really wet and slippery bridleway. With no mobile signal I struggled to locate the riding school, which I had organised previously. When I did get a signal I found out that the school was on the outskirts of Launceston, two miles away. It was entirely my fault for not plotting it properly in the first place. A little dejected, with another 45 minutes still to go, we headed off, crossed the swollen River Tamar and into Cornwall. This was to be our final county border crossing, which was poignant, as it meant the end was near. We then quickly found St Leonard's Equestrian Centre opposite Launceston Rugby Club. Abbie met us and she was in charge of the stables whilst the owner Andy was away on holiday. Marv was given a stable overlooking their outdoor school, and was able to dry out properly over-night. I was very kindly offered a holiday cottage for the night, so we both did rather well.

Day 73 (Launceston to St Cleer - 18miles)

Breakfast was a round of bacon rolls and cereal bought at the Spar the night before. The night had been very wet, and we were both lucky to have been under cover. The outdoor riding school was partially flooded. Again, I tacked him up under the available cover, and we headed off into the intermittent showers which stopped after two hours. To date on the trip, my waterproofs had not been needed much, despite this year being one of the wettest on record (I subsequently discovered).

The morning's meanderings took us through the villages of Lezant, Trebullett and Rilla Mill. As with other areas of the south west, the lanes had high hedges, so when on foot, the views were limited. The gradients were starting to tell, and were similar to a few days in the Peak district. We had a good climb up through Upton Cross to Minions on the southern edge of Bodmin Moor. Luckily, located here was a Post Office and an opportunity for snacks and photos. Waterproofs were then donned again for the final push to cross the edge of the moor. Marv became very interested in all the wild horses and ponies grazing freely around. I would have liked to have hung around a little longer for him to socialise, but the rain kept coming and we needed to get to our final destination of the day.

(L) Minions Post Office, (R) Marv spots the native ponies on the moor

We found a convenient bridleway short cut into the village of St Cleer (on the hill) and located The Stag pub. Landlord Bob had managed to secure the use of a field behind the pub, from one of his regulars Pete. Marv had plenty of grass to munch on, as this field had clearly not seen livestock for some time. I had the use of a small corrugated barn in the same field, which was full of square hay bales. This was perfect as a mattress. Bob allowed me the use of the pub shower to freshen up and an evening meal which was ideal.

I retired early to my hay loft to write my diary and catch up with Fi by phone. My bed was certainly comfortable and dry, but it was only two by two square bales wide and there was a five bale drop to the floor. I needed not to roll over in the night in my sleeping bag. Just in case I did roll, I decided to bungee myself to the side of the barn. The ever inquisitive Marv came over to see me later and stuck his head in the open door to check up on me. Small events like this really meant a great deal to me, as it did get a little lonely on the road. Though perhaps he was just checking for dry space inside should it rain?

Day 74 (St Cleer to Bugle - 18 miles)

I had a relative lie in to 0800, and woke to find Marv fast asleep in the deep grass just outside the door of the barn. I packed up my gear inside, and as soon as I was ready, Marv poked his head back in as if to say "are we off now?" He had certainly got the rhythm of the routine down to a tee. I called in at the local stores as we left the village to get some milk for my cereal which I had in a grassy layby off a tiny lane. Dried milk was something I had decided a while back not to use unless absolutely necessary. Little did I know that this was to be the day's last shop stop.

(L) Marv helps with directions, (R) nice church…

We traversed the lanes, through St Neot and Mount, came close to the outskirts of the town of Bodmin and the nearby A30 as we crossed the busy A38. Getting hungry now, I found my reserve Mars bar deep in a saddle bag, and resorted to eating dried Crunchy Nut cornflakes, which helped. We took a more scenic forest path and passed through the grounds of a National Trust property called Lanbydrock House. To exit the grounds we needed to use the pedestrian gate (next to a cattle grid) and I found this was too narrow for Marv with all his saddle bags on. So finally, learning from previous similar mistakes, I was patient and took his saddle and saddle bags off and carried them through, then led him through, to then re-tack up the other side. It may have felt like an inconvenience, but I had ripped the saddle bags too many times already by being impatient.

As it was so warm, I risked getting some sun on my back as the lanes were especially quiet. On the approach to the village of Bugle I got very clear instructions to where Barry's house and field were located. I passed a large field of caravans which apparently were to house eastern Europeans working locally. I could see the start of a huge open cast quarrying facility, which was visible for miles and dominated the entire area. This was the St Austell china clay workings, which I would have to circumnavigate tomorrow. I found Barry's house at the end of a residential cul de sac. A very unlikely place to be staying with a horse it seemed. Marv was led to a hidden field at the back of the house, this time to be sharing with a tethered goat. I was kindly offered Barry's annex which had a bed/shower/toilet facility and was ideal to do my admin in. No need for the bivi tonight.

(L) Bare arms in the sun, (R) Marv having chased the resident goat into his shed

After a short nap to recharge the batteries, I headed off to the local pub for a meal of mussels. I turned down the offer of staying for the pub quiz, and headed back to the house via the Spar for a top up of supplies and breakfast items. I checked on Marv who was being strangely competitive with the goat over territory, and was forcing the goat to go back into his little shed. I reprimanded Marv, as it was the goat's field after all. The two of them then ate peacefully together as I could see them from my annex window. I had very sore legs today and noted in my diary that I now couldn't wait to get to the finish.

Day 75 (Bugle to Trispen - 15 miles)

The weather was misty and cool today. Marv was at peace with the goat when I went to get him. I packed up and put the key for the annex through Barry's window as previously agreed, as he had left for work already. We left Bugle and passed the china clay workings. It was pleasant walking in the cool mist, although visibility was not ideal. I was concerned about our safety on the road, with cars appearing out of nowhere. We passed Roche and into Nanpean, stopping at a Post Office for some bland sandwiches and carrots for the boy. Then we continued down lanes to the outskirts of St Stephen, with even more hills to climb to reach Ladock. We had to turn around in the village and retrace our route as a set of pedestrian gates prevented Marv from getting through.

(L) Concrete block factory, (R) come on Grant, keep up…

With a final set of rollercoaster lanes completed we reached Trispen and Trevispian Vean Farm. Here, Ernie had kindly offered Marv a stable. This was to be an interesting night for the both of us. The farm was actually a massive pig farm. Marv's stable was adjacent to a barn holding at least 200 pigs. As you have probably already discovered, Marv (like many horses) had a strong aversion to pigs. Now just to put this into context, there was also a livery yard here at the farm, and there were other horses stabled only yards away. This must have given Marv some confidence that it should be safe. I did not know in advance that this was a pig farm, otherwise I would certainly have looked to stay somewhere else. It seemed rude to not stay, though this was certainly going to be a challenging night.

(L) Marv's stable window; I slept on the straw beneath it, (R) our neighbour for the night

We put the unhappy Marv in his stable and he could see (and hear) from his window the proximity of the pigs. He kept on snorting and standing at the back of his box trying to come to terms with this injustice. I decided I needed to be near him tonight, so slept on a pile of hay under his stable window. I also found that with only less than a week to go, he had a loose shoe, and so I called a kind lady called Chris (from St Newlyn East) whom I almost stayed with before straightening my route through Cornwall. She had a farrier organised within ten minutes for the following morning. Chris herself arrived later that night with some friends to see Marv, and to drop off some money she had kindly collected for the charities. Marv wasn't having a relaxing night, so I got up at midnight to reduce the size of his stable window by two slats, as I thought he was considering jumping out and escaping the pig farm altogether. He finally calmed down and we both got some rest.

Day 76 (Trispen to Ponsanooth - 11 miles)

After a stressful night for both of us, I packed up our gear and awaited the farrier who was booked for 1000. Friday the 13th (July) had already had an impact. Marv had diarrhoea (probably due to stress), and mucking him out wasn't so much fun either. We had a few well-wishing visits from Ernie, his son Nick and his wife (all of whom gave generous donations). Stephen Long the farrier, arrived slightly early and we led the tense Marv up to the hay barn to try and re-shoe him. Stephen used to be a jockey, and now trained point to pointers as well as being a farrier. He could see Marv was having trouble standing still and he was incredibly patient in re-shoeing him. He did both new rear shoes and put his fee towards the charities. A very helpful and considerate man.

(L) Stephen the farrier and Ernie, (R) ready to go for the day

We left just before 1100 and walked through the village before crossing the A39, and off again down the quiet country lanes. Fi was flying down to Exeter today, landing at 1100 and hiring a car to come and see us on our last weekend. I was keen therefore to get a move on and make up some time for our unscheduled farrier stop. We took a long track through a wood on the outskirts of Truro, and I utilised Marv's nervous energy to run a great part of it.

(L) In the woods just before Truro, (R) Truro Cathedral

Reaching the outskirts of Britain's most southerly city, I was now getting rather hungry again so I decided to travel through the city centre and grab something on route. Fiona was getting near in her hire car and we were trying to work out a suitable rendezvous to meet up. I managed a bacon roll in the pedestrianised area, and a baguette (on the house) at a deli on the way out. We paused in the city centre just long enough to get a photo of the Cathedral behind us before heading out into the countryside. We didn't have time to appreciate the sights of Truro in retrospect. Rain was lashing down as we finally met up with Fi in a service station forecourt. It was not very glamorous, but certainly functional, as it provided shelter. After a quick catch up chat and some more food for both of us, the rain stopped and Marv and I headed off for the last few miles of the day, whilst Fi went ahead to the day's stopover location.

I was met in Ponsanooth by Fi and Pam's dog Jazz (Maisie wasn't allowed to fly south), and we walked in the last few hundred metres together. Marv got a great field next to Pam's other horses; George, Willow and Lady. Freya, Pam's daughter, helped settle Marv in and get him a feed. Once he was happy, we both then went back to the Stag Inn where we were to be based for my last rest weekend. We ventured into nearby Devoran for a meal before heading back for an early night.

Day 77 (Ponsanooth - rest day)

After breakfast Fi and I went to check up on Marv before exploring nearby Falmouth. We then met up with Giles (an Army friend), his wife Ruth and kids who were holidaying in the area. We walked their dogs along the coastal path before returning to Pam's to see how Marv was enjoying his time off. Marv had managed to catch his chest with his rear shoe, probably trying to flick off flies. Giles (an Army doctor) and I administered some Hibiscrub and iodine, as it was only a minor graze. Later on, Fi and I explored the foggy Lizard Point before having dinner in Helston.

(L) Giles meets Marv, (R) Giles and Ruth on the farm

Day 78 (Ponsanooth - rest day)

We had a strategic lunch today at Victoria on the A30, as Fi had a return flight to catch to Edinburgh at 1800. Mum and Ken were arriving into Newquay (by air) at 1300. So this was to be a hand-over lunch. Fi had to go back to work sadly, and would have loved to have been at the finish as she truly deserved to be. She departed and I was driven by Mum and Ken to the Foresters B&B near St Ives where we would all be staying for the next three days until the finish.

Week 12 (34 miles)

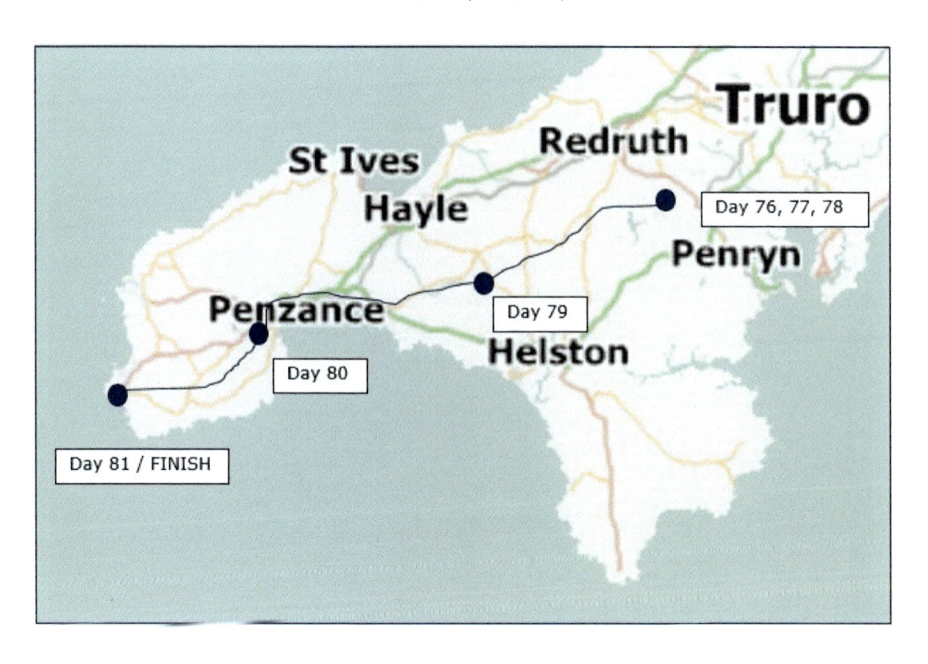

Week 12 (total 34 miles)

<u>Day 79 (Ponsanooth to Godolphin Cross - 12 miles)</u>

I had planned the last three days of the trip to be short days, lest anything go wrong I would then have a buffer to use to enable me to complete on the designated day. That day was Wednesday 18th July. So far so good, we were on plan. This was much more civilised than the twenty mile days of earlier in the trip, and it was mid-summer so the weather also helped make this a memorable finish. With this in mind, there was no rush to start the days early either, so Mum, Ken and I stopped off at the local Stithians show (largest one day show in the county apparently). There were fields of parked cars in all directions. I didn't expect to see so many people congregated in such a quiet rural area deep in Cornwall.

I headed over to the equestrian area and bought some travel boots and bandages for the return road trip. We then sat and watched some show jumping before heading over to Pam's and getting Marv ready for that day's miles. Pam and family were just saying their goodbyes to Marv as they were off to the show too. Marv and I then set off up the lanes bypassing Stithians now, and going through the villages of Carnkie and Porkellis. I met Mum and Ken near Releath and we all walked in together. Ken led Marv for much of the last few miles and therefore had to contend with Marv's verge diving activity. We met Helen, who had offered a field for Marv, at the pub in Godolphin Cross. I was initially a little disappointed to learn that the field was one mile away, very near where we had just walked past. I guess again it was my own fault for not fully clarifying the location before arrival.

(L) Mum and Ken join us for the day's miles, (R) Ken enjoying leading Marv

Pam, the field's owner, drove us round to the next village to show us where to take Marv. She had a hay net and an evening feed for him already prepared. Marv also had her horse for company tonight, and over a hundred wild rabbits helping keep the grass short. I went back to lead Marv in, as Mum and Ken had been keeping an eye on him back at the pub. After ensuring Marv was ok, we stopped at the Godolphin Arms for a quick pint before heading back to the Foresters for a shower and nipping into Penzance for a recce for tomorrow and some dinner.

Day 80 (Godolphin Cross to Newlyn - 12 miles)

Not long left now, and the weather has been kind to us. After breakfast, I was driven to Godolphin Cross and we made ready for our penultimate day's travel. Marv and I went up and over Godolphin Hill and down the lanes to the elusive coast. I had only seen the sea at the start, at Beauly, and when I crossed the Forth Road Bridge. Now with two days to go I would experience one of the most iconic beach vistas in Britain. We went through Goldwithney then into beautiful coastal Marazion. Here we saw the sea and I looked for a way down to the beach. We had a few false starts, where we couldn't make it onto the beach due to obstacles, and Marv pumped out a few loads of droppings in his excitement of seeing the sea. Maybe he hadn't been on a beach before, I just don't know, but the wind had got up and he was on his toes.

(L) Marv canters back to me at Marazion, (R) on the beach in front of St Michael's Mount

(L) On Mount Bay, (R) reaching Penzance harbour

At last we found a way onto the beach opposite the island of St Michael's Mount. I jumped up on Marv and we started cantering down the beach. I asked a friendly kite surfer to take a couple of pictures before continuing on the canter. I was quite emotionally charged, with this being a very memorable way to reach our last town. We were met by Mum and Ken, who had driven out from Penzance with a picnic which we had on the beach. Mum then left to drive to the last night's field, and Ken walked with us into the town of Penzance alongside the railway line past Britain's most southerly station. It was then through a car park and onto the quayside next to the harbour.

There were so many picture opportunities available as we passed the coastal open air salt water swimming pool and into adjoining Newlyn. There was a steep climb to contend with out of Newlyn into the amazingly discreet village of Tredavoe. Marv's last field was a cracker, with fantastic sea views and two other horses for company nearby, along with plenty of good grass. After de-kitting, we headed back to St Ives as Pete (from earlier) had arrived from Shropshire with his 4x4 and horse trailer. He had volunteered to take us back to Edinburgh the next day. The total distance he would drive to complete this would be 1150 miles, virtually the same as mine, and my profound thanks go to him for his five days out to help me conclude the trip.

I met Pete at the Foresters and we headed off for a walk round St Ives to catch up. Ken took the car to Land's End to recce the last few miles and the finish itself. We all headed out later into Marazion for a wonderful last supper overlooking St Michael's Mount, which was and still is very poignant to me.

Day 81 (Newlyn to Land's End - 10 miles)

I was up for breakfast with the finishing team of Pete, Mum and Ken, and was starting to feel a little apprehensive about the end. It was almost a year since I started planning this trip, and just over eleven weeks of having undertaken it, it was about to end today. My feelings were a mixture of: relief that it was going to be a success; pride that Marv and I had done it; pleasure that we had managed to share it with family, friends and generous strangers and sadness that this adventure was drawing to a close with all its fantastic memories.

We drove the short distance to Tredavoe, and Marv as usual trotted over to the gate, ready for the last leg. We led him down into the steading to tack him up for the last time. I then rode off on Marv up a muddy bridleway, whilst the others headed off to drop Pete's 4x4 and trailer at the finish. Marv and I did some good cross country through fields to get back onto a road and headed off towards the next rendezvous of St Buryan. I had to lead Marv over a disused cattle grid (which was filled up with soil). Marv did very well and walked over calmly. I met the team in the village, and took the opportunity to dive into the local store for some finish food for Marv to include all his favourites.

(L) Marv trots over on the last day, (R) with Pete for the last miles

Pete stayed with me, and Mum and Ken headed off for Land's End. Pete and I enjoyed the last two hours walk in to the finish, in which we kept off the busy A30 until the last possible moment whereby we had to then join it near Sennen. I climbed on board Marv to finish as we had started. The finish line was in sight, and I could see there were masses of cars parked, with Land's End itself consisting of white washed buildings clustered around the point. As we got nearer we were surprised when all the tourists started clapping, and it turned out that Ken had briefed the staff there and they had put an announcement out to everyone. So, slightly embarrassed, we trotted in to all this attention.

There was Mum and Ken at the finish with a "congratulations to Grant & Marv" banner. Jeff, the local ILPH officer was also there with his wife, as was Pam from Ponsanooth, Freya and family. I was a little overwhelmed, but chuffed to bits too. I certainly shed a tear or two in the moment. Ken opened some champagne and I was very happy to have completed the trip, but still sad that Fi and Maisie were not able to be here to share this moment with us. Without them there would have been no trip, and I have tears in my eyes as I write this now. That so many people were wishing us congratulations was a pleasant surprise. It was a fantastic end to a very special trip. There was a blue sky and glistening sea as a backdrop as Ken proposed a toast to us and to Fi, Maisie and Mark (who couldn't be there). We posed for some obligatory photos with Marv and the team, before enjoying the champagne and the moment. Pete took charge of the happy and popular Marv, feeding him constant mints and carrots as people came over to see him. A few youngsters wanted to sit on him, and I supervised this, not wanting any dramas today.

(L) The finish photo, (R) a young rider tries Marv for size

At 1500 we walked off back towards the car park, and Marv took a little encouragement to get into the trailer. You would have thought he would have run up the ramp, off for a well-earned rest. I said goodbye to Mum and Ken, who were heading back to Newquay and a flight north. It was over and I was so happy, but for me the trip would not be fully complete until we had got Marv back home.

Back to Scotland now…

Day 81 (Travel to Budleigh Salterton, Devon - 234 miles)

With Marv in the horse trailer behind, Pete and I headed off up the winding A30 to near Exeter, and our destination for tonight. We reached Budleigh Salterton Riding School early evening. This was owned by Rob, a fellow ex- King's Troop officer, and his wife Chrissie. Marv had a decent stable for the night and we shared a fish & chip supper with some beers and reminisced the night away.

Pete's transport, Marv keeps a watch out

Day 82 (Travel to Culgaith, Penrith, Cumbria - 340 miles)

We got up early and headed back to the yard from Rob's house. After mucking out, we eventually loaded Marv into the trailer and managed to say goodbye to Rob and his attentive stable staff. We headed for the M5 and the prospect of a long queue from a previous road accident. The delay wasn't too bad in the end and we reached Penrith in seven hours with Pete doing all the driving, despite me offering to share.

We were to be staying with James who I narrowly missed on my way south. He had just moved house to Newbiggin, and he had secured a field for Marv in a neighbouring village. Marv would have 130 chickens for company for the night, as well as another horse in a field the other side of a hedge. This would suit him just fine. He was well used to meeting new friends. Pete, James and I returned to the house and tried out James' recent purchase of a keenly priced inflatable hot tub set up in the garden. This was ideal for the end of a long journey. James gave us a Powerpoint presentation of his ascent of Everest before we headed out to the pub for food.

With Pete and James

Day 83 (Travel to Edinburgh - 124 miles)

We left James' at 0900 and after collecting Marv, made good time up into Scotland, arriving back in Edinburgh just after 1200. Marv was still in a huff due to all the necessary travel, to the extent of actually refusing mints and apples! We showed him into his field, which I believe he remembered from having spent four days there on his route south, many weeks ago. Pete and I were both very happy we had delivered the boy safely home after a monster trip. We could now rest easy and relax, Marv was back.

Marv back in his field, Pete looks on

Days 84 & 85 (Edinburgh)

On Saturday, we (Fi, Maisie and Pete and I) visited Marv, and he had thrown off his grump and now gladly accepted snacks. On Sunday, when we visited him with Maisie, he was still lying down. I went over and sat with him for a while whilst I fed him carrots. He nuzzled for some more, but there were none left. Marv was back to normal, and so relaxed. It was a fitting end to an incredible journey for the both of us.

ROUTE OF RIDE AND MILEAGE - 29 APRIL-18 JULY 2007
FROM JOHN O' GROATS TO LAND'S END (1085 MILES)

Day	Date Miles	From / to, including waypoints (# accommodation type)

START

Week 1 (170 miles)

1.	Sun 29 Apr 23	John o' Groats to Mybster (sofa)
2.	Mon 30 Apr 23	Mybster via Westerdale and Altnabreac railway station to Fosinard (bivi)
3.	Tue 1 May 19	Fosinard via Kinbrace and Loch Badanloch to Gearnsary bothy (bivi)
4.	Wed 2 May 21	Gearnsary bothy via Ben Armine Lodge to Rogart (b)
5.	Thu 3 May 24	Rogart via Bonar Bridge and Glen Carron to near Amat (bivi)
6.	Fri 4 May 20	Amat via Glen More, Deanich Lodge, Alladale Lodge and Strath Vaich to near Inchbae Lodge (tent)
7.	Sat 5 May 19	Inchbae Lodge via Contin and Marybank to Muir of Ord (b)
8.	Sun 6 May 21	Muir of Ord to Tomich (barn)

Accommodation type: (b) – bed; sofa; bivi; tent; caravan; barn

Week 2 (85 miles)

9.	Mon 7 May 16	Tomich to Fort Augustus (b)
10.	Tue 8 May 0	Fort Augustus (b) **REST DAY** (<u>FARRIER - 1 FRONT SET</u>)
11.	Wed 9 May 18	Fort Augustus via Corrieyairack Pass to Laggan (sofa)
12.	Thu 10 May 21	Laggan via Dalwhinnie and Drumochter to Dalnaspidal Lodge (tent)
13.	Fri 11 May 25	Dalnaspidal Lodge via Trinafour and Tummel Bridge to Tirnie Farm near Aberfeldy (b)
14.	Sat 12 May 5	Tirnie Farm to Aberfeldy (b)
15.	Sun 13 May 0	Aberfeldy (b) **REST DAY**

Week 3 (79 miles)

16.	Mon 14 May 11	Aberfeldy via Glen Cochill to Amulree (b)
17.	Tue 15 May 17	Amulree via the Sma'Glen and Glenalmond to Clathy (b)
18.	Wed 16 May 19	Clathy via Dunning and Pathstruie to Cleish (b)
19.	Thu 17 May 16	Cleish via Townhill to Masterton (near Dunfermline) (b)
20.	Fri 18 May 16	Masterton via the Forth Road Bridge, past Edinburgh Airport and Heriot Watt University to Balerno (near Edinburgh) (b)
21.	Sat 19 May 0	Edinburgh (b) **REST DAY**
22.	Sun 20 May 0	Edinburgh (b) **REST DAY**

Week 4 (106 miles)

23.	Mon 21 May	19	Balerno via the Pentland Hills, Glen Corse and Middleton to Heriot (tent)
24.	Tue 22 May	19	Heriot via Galashiels to Melrose (b)
25.	Wed 23 May	19	Melrose via St Boswells to Oxnam (b)
26.	Thu 24 May	14	Oxnam via 'Dere St', crossing into England next to Otterburn Military training area to Cottonshopeburnfoot (tent)
27.	Fri 25 May	15	Cottonshopeburnfoot via Hareshaw Head and Corsenside Common to Woodburn near Bellingham (b)
28.	Sat 26 May	20	Woodburn via Birtley, Chipchase and Haughton Castles, Walwick and Keepwick Fell to Anick near Hexham (b)
29.	Sun 27 May	0	Anick (b) **REST DAY**

Week 5 (104 miles)

30.	Mon 28 May 19	Anick via Blanchland, Townfield and Hunstanworth Moor to Rookhope (tent)
31.	Tue 29 May 20	Rockhope via Lintzgarth Common, Westgate, Swinhope Moor and Newbiggin to Middleton in Teesdale (b)
32.	Wed 30 May 16	Middleton in Teesdale <u>(FARRIER – 1 REAR SET)</u> via Selset Reservoir and Brough to Nateby near Kirby Stephen (bivi)
33.	Thu 31 May 16	Nateby via alongside Settle-Carlisle railway, Garsdale Head and Dentdale to Cowgill (b)
34.	Fri 1 June 16	Cowgill via Newby Head, Ribblehead viaduct and Horton in Ribblesdale to Stainforth near Settle (bivi)
35.	Sat 2 June 17	Stainforth via the Ribble Way and Settle, to Saltersforth near Barnoldswick (tent)
36.	Sun 3 June 0	Saltersforth (bivi) **REST DAY**

Week 6 (120 miles)

37.	Mon 4 June 19		Saltersforth via Widdop reservoir, Gorple Lower reservoir and the Pennine bridleway to Blackshaw Head (b)
38.	Tue 5 June 18		Blackshaw Head via Lumbutts, Rochdale Canal towpath, Littleborough, Hollingworth Lake, under the M62, Denshaw and Castleshaw reservoirs to Diggle (b)
39.	Wed 6 June 16		Diggle via (Pennine bridleway) Greenfield, Walkerwood Reservoir, Matley, Mottram, Broad Bottom and Charlesworth to Little Hayfield (bivi)
40.	Thu 7 June 23		Little Hayfield via (Pennine bridleway) Peak Forest to Blackwell (bivi)
41.	Fri 8 June 20		Blackwell via (Pennine bridleway), Biggin <u>(FARRIER – 1 FRONT SET)</u> to Ashbourne (caravan)
42.	Sat 9 June 23		Ashbourne via Rocester, Uttoxter and Bramshall to Kingstone (bivi)
43.	Sun 10 June 0		Kingstone (bivi) **REST DAY**

Week 7 (76 miles)

44.	Mon 11 June 23	Kingstone via under the M6, Staffs & Worcs Canal towpath, Penkridge, Brewood and Shropshire Union Canal towpath to Codsall (sofa)
45.	Tue 12 June 20	Codsall via Monarch's Way / Staffordshire Way, Pattingham and Shatterford to Trimpley (b)
46.	Wed 13 June 16	Trimpley to Martley (b)
47.	Thu 14 June 0	Martley (b) **REST DAY**
48.	Fri 15 June 0	Martley (b) **REST DAY**
49.	Sat 16 June 0	Martley (h) **REST DAY**
50.	Sun 17 June 5	Martley to Worcester (b)

Week 8 (62 miles)

51.	Mon 18 June 12		Worcester via Crowle to Radford (b)
52.	Tue 19 June 16		Radford via Evesham and Bretforton to Weston sub Edge (b)
53.	Wed 20 June 16		Weston sub Edge via Chipping Campden and Moreton in Marsh <u>(FARRIER 1 FRONT SET)</u> to Bledington (b)
54.	Thu 21 June 14		Bledington via Shipton under Wychwood and Swinbrook to Carterton (b)
55.	Fri 22 June 16		Carterton via Kencot, Langford and Lechlade to Shrivenham (b)
56.	Sat 23 June 0		Shrivenham (b) **REST DAY**
57.	Sun 24 June 0		Shrivenham (b) **REST DAY**

Week 9 (64 miles)

58.	Mon 25 June 16	Shrivenham via over the M4, the Ridgeway and Barbury Castle to Malborough (b)
59.	Tue 26 June 22	Malborough via Wilcot, Woodbridge, East Chisenbury, Longstreet, Netheravon and the Salisbury Plain to Larkhill (b)
60.	Wed 27 June 14	Larkhill via Stonehenge, Great Wishford and Dinton to Fovant (b)
61.	Thu 28 June 0	Fovant (b) **REST DAY** – trip to London, to see 60th Anniversary of the King's Troop RHA
62.	Fri 29 June 12	Fovant via South Downs to Shaftesbury (b)
63.	Sat 30 June 14	Shaftesbury via Guys March, Marnhull and Stalbridge to Purse Caundle (b)
64.	Sun 1 July 0	Purse Caundle (b) **REST DAY**

Week 10 (89 miles)

65.	Mon 2 July 0	Purse Caundle (b) **REST DAY**	
66.	Tue 3 July 17	Purse Caundle via Milborne Port, Sanford Orcas, RNAS Yeovilton and Lyles Cary to Somerton (b)	
67.	Wed 4 July 18	Somerton via Langport, Stoke St Gregory and North Curry to Creech St Michael (b)	
68.	Thu 5 July 18	Creech St Michael via under the M5, Bridgewater & Taunton Canal Towpath and Taunton to Holcombe Rogus (b)	
69.	Fri 6 July 18	Holcombe Rogus via Pennymoor and Puddington to Black Dog (bivi)	
70.	Sat 7 July 19	Black Dog via Morchard Bishop and Monkokehampton to Hatherleigh (b)	
71.	Sun 8 July 0	Hatherleigh (b) **REST DAY**	

Week 11 (86 miles)

72.	Mon 9 July 20	Hatherleigh via Bratton Clovelly and Lifton to Launceston (b)
73.	Tue 10 July 18	Launceston via Lezant, Trebullett, Rilla Mill, Upton Cross and Minions to St Cleer (barn)
74.	Wed 11 July 18	St Cleer via St Neot and Mount to Bugle (b)
75.	Thu 12 July 15	Bugle via Roche, Nanpean, St Stephen and Ladock to Trispen (barn)
76.	Fri 13 July 11	Trispen <u>(FARRIER - 1 REAR SET)</u> via Truro to Ponsanooth (b)
77.	Sat 14 July 0	Ponsanooth (b) **REST DAY**
78.	Sun 15 July 0	Ponsanooth (b) **REST DAY**

Week 12 (34 miles)

79.	Mon 16 July 12	Ponsanooth via Carnkie, Porkellis and Releath to Godolphin Cross (b)
80.	Tue 17 July 12	Godolphin Cross via Goldwithney, Marazion and Penzance to Newlyn (b)
81.	Wed 18 July 10	Newlyn via St Buryan and Sennen to Land's End

FINISH

    Total   1085 miles

To get back to Edinburgh by 4x4 and horse trailer:

81.	Wed 18 July (234 miles)	Land's End to Budleigh Salterton, Devon (b)
82.	Thu 19 July (340 miles)	Budleigh Salterton to Culgaith, Cumbria (b)
83.	Fri 20 July (124 miles)	Culgaith to Edinburgh (b)

To get to the start by horse box:

0.	Sat 28 Apr (281 miles)	Edinburgh to John o' Groats (b)

List of equipment carried

For Marv:
Saddle (Free N Easy) with lightweight plastic racing stirrups
Waterproof saddle cover
Bridle (lightweight plastic coated fabric racing type)
Head collar & rope
Reins (lightweight Army rip stop fabric tape for durability)
Saddle bags
Breastplate
Small equine medical kit – bandage, iodine spray, etc
Hoof pick / stiff dandy brush
Medi boot (not used, but carried)
Bags of D&H Staypower muesli (not required after N.Scot)
Equine Midge head cover (not required after N. Scot)
Equine midge rug (not required, dropped after wk 1)
Collapsible water carrier bucket (not required, dropped after wk 1)

For me:
Helmet (lightweight climbing variety by Petzel)
High vis vest
Lightweight waterproof jacket and trousers
Woollen hat
Gloves
Two pairs of walking trousers
Polo shirt/ 2 t-shirts
2 sets of underwear
1 sweater
1 fleece lined wind stopper jacket
4 pairs of socks
Trainers (used after Scotland)
Basic wash kit
Lightweight travel towel
Mess tin / KFS (knife,fork,spoon) / plastic mug
Small gas stove and canister / lighter
Water bottle
Lightweight sleeping bag / bivi bag
Thermarest
Poncho with bungees attached, 4 pegs
Camera
Mobile phone and charger
Emergency rations (noodles/chocolate)
Sun cream (for both Marv and I)
Fencing tool

20m spare lightweight fabric tape
Day sack
Small sewing kit
Sunglasses
Maps for each week and waterproof map case
Lightweight compass
Small head torch
Diary and route spreadsheet/contacts list
Pair of robust shorts
Fleece gilet
Flip flops
Leatherman tool

Half chaps (not used after Scotland)
Camel jodhpur boots (not used after Scotland)

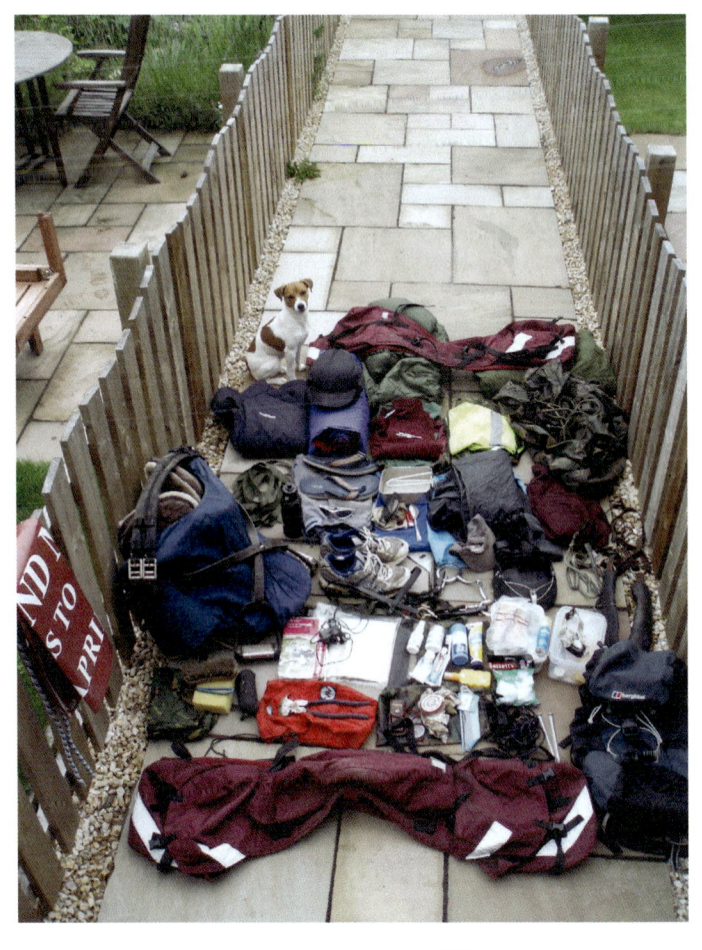

Glossary (mostly military)

AMEC	Advanced Military Equitation Course
Bombardier	Full Corporal in the Artillery
bergen	Military rucksack
BHS	British Horse Society
bivi or poncho	Military term for a waterproof sheet usually suspended by bungees attached to a fence or similar used as a shelter
bivi bag	A breathable waterproof sleeping bag shell
DAC	Defence Animal Centre (Melton Mowbray in Leicestershire)
ILPH	International League for the Protection of Horses (now WHW)
OCMTF	Officer Commanding Military Training Flight (in charge of military parachuting training)
MOD	Ministry of Defence
OS	Ordnance Survey
P Company	4 Week physically arduous course required to be completed by potential airborne forces (held in Catterick, Yorkshire)
RA	Royal Artillery
RAF	Royal Air Force
RHA	Royal Horse Artillery
RMAS	Royal Military Academy Sandhurst (Berkshire)
RMCS	Royal Military College Science (Shrivenham, Wiltshire)
Royal Mile	Centuries old cobbled road in central Edinburgh running from Holyrood Palace up to Edinburgh Castle
RSA	Royal School of Artillery (Larkhill, Wiltshire)
WHW	World Horse Welfare (formerly ILPH)
YOs	Young Officers Artillery course held at RSA
1 Para	1st Battalion the Parachute Regiment
7 Para RHA	7th Parachute Regiment Royal Horse Artillery

Acknowledgements for the trip

Fi (and Maisie) for everything

Mark for the website and the John o' Groats drop off

Julian for assisting in editing the diary

Mum and Ken for all their support

The ILPH for their overall support and visits from ILPH local field officers during the trip

All the generous people, family and friends who allowed me and Marv to stay en route, and friends who met up with us and shared in a leg of the trip

Donations for the charities during the journey, and donations of money made via the Justgiving website, including many thousand pounds raised by my sister Sarah. Just over £10,000 was raised in total, split roughly 50/50 between the two charities.

To all the superb farriers who at very little notice went out of their way to keep Marv shod wherever we happened to be

Pete for the Land's End pick up and monster drive home

Acknowledgements for the book

Fi again for her transcript of my daily diary scribbles which was used as a fundamental skeleton for the book

Janice, Douglas, Bev and Derek for their invaluable editing

Amy Williams for her Foreword.

Printed in Poland
by Amazon Fulfillment
Poland Sp. z o.o., Wrocław